T0402545

FOLLOWING NATURE'S LEAD

Following Nature's Lead

ANCIENT WAYS OF LIVING IN A
DYING WORLD

M. D. USHER

PRINCETON UNIVERSITY PRESS

PRINCETON & OXFORD

Published by Princeton University Press
41 William Street, Princeton, New Jersey 08540
99 Banbury Road, Oxford OX2 6JX

press.princeton.edu

GPSR Authorized Representative: Easy Access System Europe - Mustamäe tee 50, 10621 Tallinn, Estonia, gpsr.requests@easproject.com

All Rights Reserved

Library of Congress Cataloging-in-Publication Data

Names: Usher, M. D. (Mark David), 1966– author.
Title: Following nature's lead: ancient ways of living in a dying world / M. D. Usher.
Description: Princeton: Princeton University Press, 2025 | Includes bibliographical references and index.
Identifiers: LCCN 2024034975 | ISBN 9780691249209 (hardback) | ISBN 9780691249612 (ebook)
Subjects: LCSH: Philosophy of nature. | Philosophy, Ancient. | Civilization, Modern—Ancient influences. | BISAC: PHILOSOPHY / Environmental | NATURE / Environmental Conservation & Protection
Classification: LCC BD581.F785 2025 | DDC 113—dc23/eng/ 20241202
LC record available at https://lccn.loc.gov/2024034975

British Library Cataloging-in-Publication Data is available

Jacket image: Pakorn Preechaphong / Shutterstock

This book has been composed in Arno

Printed in Canada

10 9 8 7 6 5 4 3 2 1

Progress may have been all right once, but it went on too long.

—OGDEN NASH (1902–1971)

CONTENTS

List of Illustrations ix

Preface: "A Book for All and None" xi

Acknowledgments xix

Introduction: "Nothing Comes from Nothing" 1

1 "What Chemistry!" 14

2 "There Are Gods Here Too" 45

3 "Cosmos Out of Chaos" 87

4 "THERE IS NO WEALTH BUT LIFE" 124

Taking Stock: An Epilogue 171

Notes 179

Index 193

ILLUSTRATIONS

0.1. Bust of Epicurus (second century CE).　4

0.2. William Dyce (1806–1864), *King Lear and the Fool in the Storm*.　9

1.1. Sandro Botticelli (1445–1510), *Venus and Mars*.　18

1.2. Liebig's Barrel.　31

1.3. Gnōthi Sauton ("Know Thyself"), Baths of Diocletian, Rome, ca. first century CE.　39

1.4. "Mistress of the Animals," Çatalhöyük, Turkey, ca. 6000 BCE.　41

2.1. *Argas persicas*, scientific drawing of a female tick.　58

2.2. The electromagnetic spectrum.　61

2.3. Wheeler's rendering of the Participatory Anthropic Principle.　69

2.4. Hierocles's Circles of Concern.　83

2.5. Hierocles's Circles with eudaimonic virtues and material services inscribed.　84

3.1. A textbook illustration of the Earth's evolutionary timeline.　91

3.2. The Seneca Curve. 102

3.3. "Death by hockey sticks." 103

3.4. Herbert Wendell Gleason, *The Fitchburg Railroad and Walden Pond in Winter, Concord, Mass.*, March 24, 1920. 106

3.5. Herbert Wendell Gleason, *Sand Foliage from Deep Cut on R.R. (Railroad), Concord, Mass.*, March 17, 1900. 107

4.1. The Ecological Pyramid. 128

4.2. Tlingit potlatch at Sitka, Alaska, 1904, Haines Sheldon Museum. 141

4.3. John Ruskin, *Self-portrait in Blue Neckcloth*, 1875. 147

4.4. John Ruskin's personal seal and motto "To-day." 169

E.1. Jean-Baptiste Chardin (1699–1779), *Soap Bubbles.* 177

"A Book for All and None"

WHAT OF VALUE can the study of classical literature, history, and philosophy contribute to the modern world's ecological and economic challenges? Are older ways of thinking and living worth our time to consider, or to reconsider? Are they viable modes of engagement with the world today?

I think so, and the following pages aim to explain how and why.

It is tempting to say, given its premise, that this is a book for everyone and no one, but that would be to claim too much for it. It is not, at any rate, an academic book. There are, for example, no footnotes, and no fine print. But scholars and specialists are warmly invited to read it with open hearts and minds with the understanding that what I present here is just one interpretation of things—my interpretation—and so perhaps an idiosyncratic one. If asked to imagine an ideal reader I would say it would be an ordinary person who's looking for a change of perspective that is at once personal and systemic, whose concern is both local and global. I hope you exist. And I hope I will have said something here to pique your interest.

I described an earlier book I wrote in a similar vein as a collection of essays—essays in the etymological sense: "forays," "ventures," "attempts." The chapters included here are perhaps more akin to sermons. Not that I am preaching a creed, but because I take ancient scriptures as my point of departure and try to offer what I hope is an edifying contemporary message (and perhaps just a touch of fire and brimstone). While the focus is on classical antiquity, this book covers other terrain as well, with much else at the margins and in between. It concerns philosophy, poetry, and religion, but also economics and science. It seeks to clarify, conceptually and experientially, what that shibboleth "sustainability" could possibly mean on a planet that might well be beyond its tipping point. It speaks from experience, too (twenty-plus years of smallholding and homesteading in Vermont). Thus, inevitably, these musings also amount to a confession about the contingencies, trade-offs, failures, and rewards of trying to live authentically and think ecologically in a dying, yet dynamic world.

Why classics? Quite simply it is the field in which I hoe my beans. But there are other reasons, too, that will emerge as things proceed. Are there other ancient ways to live in a dying world? Yes. Indigenous ways. Confucian ways. Islamic ways. The Taoist Way. Buddhist ways. Vedic ways. If there is a bias or folly in my approach, it consists in a tendency to admire traditions of many sorts. On this point an observation by G. K. Chesterton, who was partial to the Judeo-Christian way, provides, I think, a compelling rationale:

Tradition means giving votes to the most obscure of all classes, our ancestors. It is the democracy of the dead. Tradition refuses to submit to the small and arrogant oligarchy of those who merely happen to be walking about. All democrats object to people being disqualified by the accident of birth; tradition objects to their being disqualified by the accident of death.

If we wish to be truly pluralistic and fully democratic thinkers, we should acknowledge, steely eyed, the sociocultural evolution that has brought human communities to this point in time, and, amid the clamor of contemporary voices that assails us every day, listen also to those who still speak across the ages. If the word "tradition," or the verdict of a White, Roman Catholic male presents a stumbling block, consider the Anarchists' view on ownership, which speaks differently to the same point. Ownership, they argue, is a legal fiction. We are not the sole proprietors of any property we might happen to possess. A parcel of land, for example, has been molded and improved by many hands over centuries. So has a house. New technologies and gadgets are dependent on prior innovations and labor contributed by others. New ideas spring from existing knowledge. "All," Kropotkin writes, "belongs to all."

When it comes specifically to living with Nature, Indigenous traditions are particularly instructive. Shared ancestral knowledge in Indigenous communities is place-based, relationship-focused, situated in narrative, relationally accountable, and actionable. And yet the same is largely true of the Greco-Roman tradition, which is preserved for the most part via narratives (myths, history, philosophy) in which actionable appeal is constantly being made to the *mos maiorum* ("the custom of the ancestors") and to autochthony ("nativeness"; literally, "being self-sprung from the soil").

Premodernity, it seems, speaks a *lingua franca*. From the vantage point of the species, it is not an exaggeration or a slight to say that everyone is indigenous; or, given humans' long prehistory of migration—down from the trees, across the savannahs of Africa, now to every corner of the globe—none of us are. At the very least—identity politics and reparations for historical mistreatment notwithstanding—if we want to thrive together on this planet, we should consider ourselves indigenous and live accordingly. The world is fortunate that actual Indigenous traditions still exist to bear witness to how we might do that. We'll have more to say about this later.

One might be quick to object that traditions—all traditions, not just Western ones—are replete with examples of violence, oppression, injustice, persecution, and hypocrisy. That's certainly true. But the actors and institutions of the past are no more disqualified from consideration on that score alone than is our present age. In fact, the old adage that the more things change, the more they stay the same still rings truer than it should. And while of course what we owe the future must also inform our individual and collective decisions, I worry that Longtermism, as it's known, and its ethical corollary, Effective Altruism, are not as long-term or effective a view as we need. At its best, Longtermism amounts to a tyranny of a few people in the present making decisions for billions of people in the future, whose needs, best interests, and preferences might be quite different than we imagine. As for Effective Altruism, insofar as it recommends "earning to give"—that is, that you make as much money as you can so that you can give a bunch of it away and have done with your duty—it is an outlook that is predicated on the biospheric impossibility of ever-expanding economic growth and the acquisition and accumulation of ever-greater wealth. No wonder it's Elon Musk's philosophy of choice. The collapse of cryptocurrency speculator Sam Bankman-Fried, another (now former) billionaire enthusiast, shows just how precarious a solution it is. As a certain Yogi once put it, the future ain't what it used to be.

To look to philosophies of the past for clues on how to live, by contrast, involves contraction—like a muscle flexing itself—and seems to me a rather ecological approach, as it represents a repurposing, or upcycling, if you will, of proven materials we already have close to hand. It, too, concerns the future: When a reporter once asked Gandhi what he thought of Western civilization, he replied that it would be a good idea. The jury, in other words, is still out. The votes are still being counted, even as we are running out of time. Ultimately, though, my aspiration in enfranchising the past is perhaps best expressed by the Marquis de Vauvenargues, a friend of Voltaire's and a pert epigrammatist, who once quipped that "A truly new and truly original book would be one that made people fall in love with old truths." To that end my efforts here.

———

A word about the word Nature: I prefer to capitalize it. Nature is of course a slippery term and concept. By capitalizing, I do not mean to essentialize. Rather, I'm invoking Nature as a category and inviting readers to impute connotations of meaning for themselves depending on context, relying on their own familiarity with the debate, and by following the evidence/arguments presented in these pages. That the world's preeminent journal of scientific research, founded in 1869, still calls itself *Nature* inspires confidence in this matter. A good working definition and what I usually mean by Nature might be: "processes and preconditions in the nonhuman world as observed and experienced by humans, especially as discovered by scientific investigation."

But, of course, humans themselves are also part and parcel of Nature. A now canonical collection of essays curated by William Cronon, *Uncommon Ground: Rethinking the Human Place in Nature*, brought the ambivalences of our relationship to the natural world uniquely to the fore in 1996. In Cronon's own contribution to that volume, "The Trouble with Wilderness; or, Getting Back to the Wrong Nature," he criticizes a false and fruitless dualism in contemporary culture that pits pristine wilderness against human communities, the one deemed pure and unspoiled, the other an inevitable perpetrator of ecological destruction and demise. His conclusion is that "We mistake ourselves when we suppose that wilderness can be the solution to our culture's problematic relationships with the nonhuman world." The tree in our backyard is just as majestic and precious as one in the forest primeval. The plant pots on our porches reproduce in microcosm the biophysical realities that make all Life possible.

I couldn't agree more. Nature is a historically conditioned, polyvalent concept that, because it includes humans, is necessarily of intrinsic concern to people living in both urban and rural environments. The motto of the city of Chicago, *urbs in horto* ("a city set in a garden"), illustrates this proposition nicely. Chicago is a sprawling metropolis that boasts ample green spaces, hence the motto. But the idea behind the phrase is also metaphorical, that urban living can respond with symbiotic sensitivity to natural settings, including mental landscapes that embrace lifestyles lived in cooperation with Nature. In whatever way we understand or experience it, Nature is, in the end, inescapably, our collective destiny since the biosphere is the ultimate source of any attempt to live ecologically meaningful lives—or indeed to live at all—be it in a dive on Division Street or on a farm in Fayette County. At that larger scale, both the problem and the possibilities could not be more urgent. The late Bruno Latour hit the nail on the head when he observed, "What happened to the landscape, for earlier generations, is now happening to the whole Earth: its gradual artificialization is making the notion of 'nature' as obsolete as that of 'wilderness.'" Which is reason enough, I should think, to try to get back to it, and learn to follow its lead.

ACKNOWLEDGMENTS

TO ACKNOWLEDGE my intellectual and practical debts to others is a pleasure, but no small task, as I have many. Here is a summary IOU.

Socrates told the jurors at his trial that one of the best things about being dead, should there be an afterlife, is the prospect of conversing with great heroes from the past. Ajax and Odysseus were near the top of his list. Near the top of mine, certainly among the recent dead, stands the great French classicist and philosopher Pierre Hadot, who lurks like a friendly ghost at the corner of every page of this book. Hadot did us all a great service in reminding the modern world that ancient philosophy, of whatever stripe, was never just a set of veridical propositions, a mental exercise, a puzzle, a problem, or a game, but a way of life that demanded the reorientation of one's whole person and, as needs must, a rejection of conventional values. His *Philosophy as a Way of Life* and *What Is Ancient Philosophy?* are the books to pick up should you choose to put this one down. Along with his final work, *The Veil of Isis: An Essay on the History of the Idea of Nature*, Hadot's *oeuvre* remains the definitive primer to what it might mean to follow Nature's lead. But I take courage from a fellow American, Emerson, who says in "The American Scholar," a lecture delivered at Harvard hard on the heels of his own great sermon on Nature from 1836, that every age must write its own books, so, *voilà*, here is mine.

Other debts and influences: to the French Institute for Advanced Study at Fondation IMéRA (Aix-Marseille University) for a generous residency fellowship in 2021–2022, which was funded by a Marie Skłodowska-Curie international mobility award, an initiative of the European Union's Horizon 2020 research and innovation program; to the University of Vermont for granting a research leave that enabled me to accept that fellowship; to Caroline, my *l'âme sœur*, for doing all the farm chores while I was away and for so much else besides (my life-debt to you, you amazing woman, is literally incalculable); to Rob Tempio, publisher *extraordinaire* at Princeton University Press; to Dominique Bourg, his Swiss counterpart, along with Sophie Swaton at Fondation Zoein and Paul Garapon of Presses universitaires de France, which is simultaneously publishing this book in French—*un grand merci*; to Thierry Fabre, a modern Montaigne, with a Mediterranean splash of Camus mixed in; to Richards twain—Martin and Seaford—for inspiration and support, and, likewise, Brendan Fisher; and to Sabine Luciani, Pierluigi Lanfranchi, and Anne Balansard of Aix-Marseille University and Carlos Lévy (the Sorbonne) for an exhilarating workshop on the topic of this book (same to seminar organizers and participants at the Macmillan Center Program in Agrarian Studies at Yale). Ca' Foscari University in Venice gave me the opportunity to present my ideas on Ruskin and Bataille (gratitude especially to Emma Sdegno). To dear friends from IMéRA: Samia Henni and Pascal Schwaighofer, Lino and Varvara Camprubí, Samuel Sami Everett, Francesca Cagnacci, Chris Shisanya, and all the other fellows, research directors, and staff;

at UVM: to new colleagues in the Department of Geography and Geosciences, old friends from Classics, and to the Environmental Program, the Food Systems Graduate Program, and the Gund Institute for Environment for joyous, ongoing affiliations. Others: Ben McCall; Nate Sanders; Luke Parker; James Bradley Wells; Joshua Brown; Don Ross; Tom Murphy; Chloe Coy; Joëlle Delbourgo; Jesse Lundquist. All of you are absolved of any errors or misjudgments contained herein, but you can certainly take some of the credit for anything good.

On matters of citation, I have avoided quoting passages in their original languages and employ key Greek and Latin words and phrases only sparingly. I can vouch, though, that my engagement with primary sources is firsthand, as all translations, unless otherwise noted, are my own. References to the ancient and modern sources that inform my thinking are gathered at the back of the book by chapter as unnumbered endnotes. These entries do not amount to a bibliography, as my goal was never to be comprehensive or authoritative and I was eager to avoid unnecessary eyesores for everyday readers. Scholars, I decided, will have the wherewithal to find what they need to verify or dispute a claim in the back matter or elsewhere should they so wish.

Credit for images accrues as follows:

0.1. Metropolitan Museum of Art, Rodgers Fund, 1911.
0.2. National Gallery of Scotland.
1.1. The National Gallery, London.
1.2. Image courtesy of David Harrod.
1.3. Michael Hurst, 2011.
1.4. Nevit Dilmen 2012, CC BY-SA 3.0.

2.1. Colored drawing by A. J. E. Terzi, Wellcome Collection, CC BY 4.0.

2.2. Image courtesy of William Neff. Image appears in Joel Achenbach, "NASA Unveils First Images from James Webb Space Telescope," *Washington Post*, July 11, 2022.

2.3. *Quantum Theory and Measurement*, edited by John Archibald Wheeler and Wojciech Hubert Zurek, Princeton University Press, 2016.

2.4. Image courtesy of Kai Whiting.

2.5. Image courtesy of Kai Whiting.

3.1. LadyofHats, 2012, CC0 1.0.

3.2. Image courtesy of Ugo Bardi.

3.3. Image courtesy of Tom Murphy.

3.4. Courtesy of the Concord Free Public Library.

3.5. Courtesy of the Concord Free Public Library.

4.1. Swiggity.Swag.YOLO.Bro, 2015, CC BY-SA 4.0.

4.2. Artstor, Visual Arts Legacy Collection.

4.3. Robert Hewison, 2000.

4.4. *Library Edition of the Complete Works of John Ruskin*, edited by E. T. Cook and Alexander Wedderburn, George Allen, 1903–1912.

E.1. Los Angeles County Museum of Art.

FOLLOWING NATURE'S LEAD

Introduction

"NOTHING COMES FROM NOTHING"

BRUNO LATOUR, among the foremost philosophers and sociologists of science in his generation, argued that to untangle the intricate yet urgent problem of human beings' environmental impact on the planet will require "sensitivity," which he defines in terms of systems science as "detecting and reacting rapidly to small changes, influences, signals." Organisms that lack such sensitivity, as evolutionary processes make abundantly clear, do not survive. Ancient peoples, despite all their pillaging and plundering, had an advantage over us in this regard: They were preindustrialized. They were predigital. They were precapitalist, prereductionist, prepostmodern, preposthuman. Of necessity they lived closer and with greater sensitivity to both the perils and the prospects of their environments. Innocent of our technology-enhanced disconnectedness from Nature, the Greeks and the Romans, like their Mediterranean neighbors, retained an earthiness and proximity to the sources of their survival that most people living in highly industrialized countries no longer possess today. As heirs to their estate—and in today's Westernized world all peoples are in some sense inheritors—we have much to relearn from them, and not only from their mistakes.

Here's an example of what I mean that is indicative of many other suggestions offered up over the course of this book.

In a recent paper, noted environmental philosopher J. Baird Callicott argues that to achieve socioeconomic sustainability in terms consistent with the Earth's biogeochemical cycles requires that we follow Nature's example: "Ecological sustainability," he writes, "is a matter of adapting human economic systems to and modeling them on the economy of nature in which the globalized human economy is embedded and in relation to which it should stand as microcosm to macrocosm." Insofar as Nature's economy runs on solar energy and all of Nature's elemental substrates—hydrogen, oxygen, carbon, nitrogen, and so on—are recycled, the human economy, Callicott argues, will only be sustainable with respect to Nature if it is a dynamic but closed-loop system, powered by solar energy, in which all materials are reabsorbed or dissipated such that there is no non-biodegradable waste.

The argument is a page out of Lucretius.

Lucretius was an Epicurean, whose cosmology pictured everything in the universe as comprised of tiny particles called atoms. The cornerstone of Epicurean physics, upon which its ethics were also based, is the doctrine sprung from empirical demonstration that "nothing comes from nothing or returns to nothing." Earth's life cycles, Lucretius argues throughout his poem, the *De Rerum Natura*, provide ample proof of this postulate. "Whatever you see," he sings, "does not wholly pass away, since Nature re-creates one thing from another and does not allow anything to be born except that fostered by the death of something else." In the language of modern science, what Lucretius is describing here and throughout his poem is an early adumbration of the Law of the Conservation of Energy as it unfolds in photosynthesis and other biogeochemical systems. But growth and decay are also phenomena ordinary observers in the agrarian societies of antiquity would have seen transpiring every day. Lucretius's handling of this topic—and his poem teems with examples drawn from agricultural *milieux*—might thus be more aptly described with a correspondingly humbler phrase—the philosophy of compost—by which is meant an understanding of closed-loop systems that involve symbiotic interrelationships between landscapes, plants, animals, and humans in which nothing is ultimately lost in the process of organic transfer.

Callicott's idea, it turns out, is old.

Lucretius's scientific reasoning reflects a typical ancient way of thinking—of inferring from Nature's observable processes what our human disposition and course of action should be. Nature, on this view, far from being red in tooth and claw, provides us with a template for living, and scientific knowledge of its workings offers consolation for the psychic banes of existence. Lucretius himself minces no words on this point: "The mind's darkness and dread must be dispelled," he insists—not by shafts of light from divine revelation or by feats of positive thinking, but "by the outward form and inward laws of Nature."

Lucretius's empiricism is a species of analogy, but one might justly call it also, in more modern parlance, a form of biomimicry. It certainly reflects the kind of sensitivity that Latour has in mind. This style of thinking, prescientific in and of itself, remains useful and has practical, ethical, and indeed scientific value for

FIGURE 0.1. Bust of Epicurus (second century CE).

us today. If nothing else, Lucretius's investigative method can and should disabuse us of our blind, uncritical allegiance to presentism. From his perspective as a nuclear physicist, J. Robert Oppenheimer once weighed its benefits in these terms:

> Analogy is indeed an indispensable and inevitable tool for scientific progress. . . . I do not mean metaphor; I do not mean allegory; I do not even mean similarity; but I mean a

special kind of similarity which is the similarity of structure, the similarity of form, the similarity of constellation between two sets of structures, two sets of particulars, that are manifestly very different, but have structural parallels.

This book concerns what is arguably the mother of all analogies—the relationship of parts to systemic whole, of human beings to the biosphere and, indeed, to the universe. All schools of ancient philosophy based their arguments on the premise that human behavior should align with states of affairs found in Nature, a principle epitomized by Latin authors with the catchphrase *secundum naturam*—"following Nature's lead"—the title of this book. In choosing how to live, work, and interact on an imperiled planet it is imperative that we do the same.

Of course, our scientific understanding of the natural world is much better now than it was in antiquity, and so our ethical positions and behavioral responses should be adjusted accordingly. On the other hand, the consequences of scientific and technological interventions today are also greater, precisely because our understanding is better (and yet still imperfect and incomplete). One might say those consequences are, potentially, exponential, for good and for ill. But lifestyles and social practices that aim to mesh harmoniously with natural systems could save us from ourselves in this regard. Ancient ways of being in the world just might provide the counterbalance we need to find a productive alternative to unlimited technological, economic, and scientific growth.

What counts as ancient is of course in the eye of the beholder. For some people the 1990s are ancient history. I find that ideas from a few generations or even a few hundred years ago are often as fresh and even more relevant today than when they were first formulated, so, in addition to the usual roster of classical writers, other oldies that fall into the tradition of following Nature loom large in this book. In my view, the actual source of a beneficial idea, whether ancient or modern, is of no consequence. Ultimately, what we should all be after is a shared way of life that manages to embrace the plurality and diversity of the world we inhabit, while respecting and preserving the processual unity of Nature.

A climate emergency, however, threatens to prevent us from realizing those or any other ideals. Judging by the data on where we're at versus where we need to be with climate mitigation, the problem seems intractable. "We are on a pathway to global warming of more than double the 1.5-degree (Celsius; or 2.7 degrees Fahrenheit) limit that was agreed to in Paris in 2015" is the United Nations' official assessment. Lucretius's maxim "nothing comes from nothing" speaks to that impending disaster, too. Shakespeare's *King Lear* offers surprising testimony. The play is littered with overt allusions to the Lucretian tag, where its meaning is ironic in that it is used to describe human motivations and actions, not biogeochemical processes. In Lucretius the already paradoxical idea (with its confounding double-negative) serves as a sound-bite to convey a natural law of physics. In the Bard's hands it becomes a vehicle for exploring the all-too-human inability to see things clearly, interpret them correctly, and act appropriately. The parallels to our contemporary predicament are nearly exact.

King Lear is an old man, set in his ways, who has ears to hear only what he wants. Throughout the play he therefore constantly misinterprets what's really going on around him, seeing "nothing" as "something" and vice versa. Shakespeare announces this pervasive motif in the play's opening scene, where Cordelia, Lear's youngest, unmarried daughter, is asked to elaborate on her filial love for him as her sisters Regan and Goneril have done just prior with effusive speeches. What's at stake is the division of Lear's kingdom among the three. When it's Cordelia's turn and Lear asks "what can you say to draw a third more opulent than your sisters? Speak." Cordelia's reply takes him aback: "Nothing, my lord." "Nothing!" Lear explodes, to which Cordelia repeats meekly, "Nothing." "Nothing will come of nothing," her father retorts with the Lucretian allusion. "Speak again."

By "nothing" Cordelia means that she has nothing to add in words that she does not already feel or has not already shown in deeds, and that she demurs from engaging in an exercise of disingenuous flattery. (We soon learn that Regan and Goneril really think their father to be a senile buffoon and scheme throughout the play to use their newly inherited power to marginalize him and increase their and their husbands' fortunes.) Lear regards Cordelia's answer as impertinent and implies she will get "nothing" of the kingdom in return for her "nothing" of praise. Despite a subsequent, sincere profession of her love, Lear disinherits her:

LEAR
So young, and so untender?
CORDELIA
So young, my lord, and true.
LEAR
Let it be so; thy truth, then, be thy dower.

Lear, however, is spooked by this fraught exchange, and the simmering pot of nothing boils over again and again throughout the play, notably in an encounter between Lear, the Earl of Kent, and Lear's court jester, the Fool. The nameless Fool, whose job it is to speak truth to power, as Cordelia herself has done, sings a ditty about wise kingship to take Lear's mind off his troubles, to which Kent replies, "This is nothing, fool." "Then 'tis like the breath of an unfee'd lawyer," the Fool parries, "You gave me nothing for't. Can you make no use of nothing, nuncle?" "Why, no, boy," Lear replies, recalling his words to Cordelia, "nothing can be made out of nothing."

Later, as the plot thickens, and the King descends into full-blown madness brought on by his elder daughters' betrayals and regret for his own mistreatment of innocent Cordelia, Lear and his Fool find themselves wandering blindly on the moor, caught in a violent storm. The wind and rain singe the King's gray head, Shakespeare says, making "nothing" of it. Whereupon Cordelia's words surface again to haunt him: Defeated, but still defiant, Lear tries to calm himself and resolves, against all foes: "No, I will be the pattern of all patience; I will say nothing." By the end of the play, however, all the members of his house now dead, nothing really does arise from nothing: Holding Cordelia's corpse in his arms Lear mourns her, wailing

> No, no, no life?
> Why should a dog, a horse, a rat, have life,
> And thou no breath at all? Thou'lt come no more,
> Never, never, never, never, never!

What, you might wonder, does any of this have to do with rising global temperatures and environmental devastation in the modern world?

FIGURE 0.2. William Dyce (1806–1864), *King Lear and the Fool in the Storm*.

In *Lear*, Shakespeare transforms Lucretius's scientific theory that nothing comes from nothing into an affective one, suggesting thereby that human interpersonal actions and reactions comprise a feedback loop that can take on tragically cosmic proportions on the world's stage. In the Age of the Anthropocene, we now know that human activity does take on such proportions, to the detriment of the biosphere, its plants and animals, and human well-being. We tend to blame trains, planes, and automobiles for our climate predicament. But, as in *Lear*, it's really misplaced human wants and desires—that is, emotional, psychological impulses—and errors of judgment and overreach—that are the sources of catastrophe.

Because we want to, and because we can, and because we misjudge outcomes, modern humans have created a situation wherein we are now dangerously dependent on machines and complex devices, to build and operate which we must extract and expend vast amounts of carbon and stored sunlight from the Earth in the form of fossil fuels and precious metals. Our resulting environmental "crisis" is really a long-festering malaise rooted in defective outlooks and priorities. It is not, as Garrett Hardin articulated forcefully in his classic essay from 1968, "The Tragedy of the Commons," a problem caused by technology, and thus not a problem amenable to a technological solution, even though technology has its part to play. To fix things will require changes in human behavior and values. Literature, philosophy, the arts, religion—what are called "the humanities" for good reason—have been addressing the anthropological problems that have precipitated our current regime long before the caustic industries and technologies we now possess and proliferate without restraint even existed. Shakespeare's appropriation of Lucretius's slogan is a powerful allegory for our times.

Fortunately, climate scientists are beginning to take the human element seriously and are attempting to incorporate it into their models. A recent comment piece in the journal *Nature*, for example, offers eight "insights" that enjoy strong disciplinary consensus among political scientists and economists that, if factored into climate models, would increase their usefulness to real-world policy decisions and investments. The thread running through all eight is debunking the "oversimplified logic that people are rational optimizers of scarce resources." "In reality," the authors insist, "human choice is a darker brew of misperception and missed opportunity, constrained by others' decisions"—a point not lost on Shakespeare. While it is true that creating more responsive, accurate models based on such constraints—

politicians beholden to the whims of their constituents, for example, or corporations answerable to their profit-seeking investors—will help us better assess the current and future state of the climate, the problem remains that human beings are not rational optimizers of scarce resources. Or at least too many of us aren't. Until human behavior changes in a meaningful way on a meaningful scale, through education, reflective introspection, and social coercion, the only thing more accurate models will show us is the urgent need to, well, modify our behavior. And to do that we need different values. One way to get a new set of values—a rather ecological one, I would say—is to dust off and refurbish the best of the old ones.

———

Shakespeare invokes Lucretian atomism to portray and explain the fall of the troubled house of Lear. "House" in this context is no dead metaphor: "ecology," "ecosystem," "economy"—each is derived from the Greek word *oikos*, which means "house" or "household." Indeed, Callicott's proposal to model the human economy on Nature's economy recalls the title of Linnaeus's study of ecology from 1749, the *Oeconomica Naturae*, which was itself inspired by approaches to natural philosophy pioneered in ancient Greece and Rome. It is sound science to say, as Aristotle once put it, that Nature is in fact "economical"—thrifty even—like a good housekeeper. We, too, then, if we want to follow Nature's lead, should put our house in order by perceiving clearly, judging rightly, and acting ecologically, mindful of all aspects of our domestic arrangement with the cosmos. Perhaps after experiencing the home confinements foisted upon us over the past few years by the COVID-19 pandemic we are now in a better position to respond to this line of thinking. Latour, at least, was hopeful on this point:

> We can't escape anymore, but we can inhabit the same place in a different way . . . based on the new ways of *placing ourselves differently* in the same spot. Isn't that the best way, anyway, to sum up the experience of the lockdown? Everyone started to live *at home* but *in a different way*.

But another question still looms: *why* should we do any of this?

On the one hand, the idea that nothing comes from nothing or returns to nothing in Nature can provide psychic defense against existential anxiety about annihilation and extinction, as it did for the Epicureans. All organic matter, in this view, including human beings, will be, as it were, born again, or reincarnated, or—my metaphor of preference—composted into new forms of life, with nothing to fear upon dissolution. But the scientific fact remains that in the larger scheme of things the whole Earth and its systems is dying, and nothing we can possibly dream up and no amount of good will can change that outcome. The Sun will eventually run out of energy, like billions of stars before it, expand into a red giant, and consume the Earth. It's called entropy, and it, too, is an aspect of Nature. The subtitle of this book, *Ancient Ways of Living in a Dying World*, pays this sobering natural law its due. To say that, though, is not an expression of pessimism. To the contrary, I see it as heady optimism, even idealism, to face the reality of impermanence philosophically and to come up with good reasons to live in harmony with Nature, nonetheless.

The usual rationale for climate action is to "save" the planet by reversing global warming. We most certainly should take decisive, impactful action to mitigate and potentially reverse the damage we have caused. There are strong instrumental and deontic reasons for doing so. But save the planet *for what* exactly? To preserve the socioeconomic *status quo* that brought us up to this brink? To go on enjoying the affluent, exploitative lifestyles we currently pursue, or aspire to? So the haves can keep having more and the have-nots somehow find less reason to complain about it? The "for what" question, thus, is all important, and any calculus to fix our problems must factor in the biological, ecological, and ontological necessity of death by embracing an ethos that takes seriously a consideration of whole systems.

This is a tall order, impossible perfectly to achieve. But we should feel emboldened by Lucretius and *King Lear*. *Nothing comes from nothing—or returns to nothing*. Nature is finite and perishable, but also resilient. Change, the only constant in the universe, churns on and on like a great wheel though space and time. The human imaginaries of times past, like spokes adjoining at the hub, form part of that perpetual motion. Whether we like it or not, things will come full circle. Our world of stunning yet precarious complexity is destined at some point for recalibration, as surely as all growth in Nature, once it's reached its apex, must fall to decline. A Great Simplification awaits, and the wisest course of action is to prepare for it, individually and collectively. Old ideas can help us here, as the following sermons conspire to convince you.

1

"What Chemistry!"

GROWTH AND DECAY; life and death; how to thrive on a planet that is governed by inexorable laws. These were central concerns for Lucretius, whose dictum "nothing comes from nothing or returns to nothing" serves, we have seen, as both a salve for salubrious living and an unadorned declaration of atomic fact. To align one's expectations, aspirations, and desires to the natural order of the universe, Lucretius argues, is the only way to live free from futility and fear. That conviction is such an old and stubborn philosophical idea, not unique to the Epicureans, that it pops up in the most unlikely of places. René Descartes, for example, at whose feet is usually laid blame for the Mind–Matter dualism that has alienated modern human beings from their natural environments, declares in the very treatise where he articulates those ideas, the *Discourse on the Method* (1637), that one of his fundamental rules for living is nonetheless, as he puts it, "to change my desires, not the order of the world."

For Lucretius, the physical world came into being by chance, the result of random collisions of atoms falling through empty space. One might think a universe without teleological purpose at its origin might also be perceived as without meaning, but for the Epicureans this was far from the case. On the contrary, the atomic structure of all life offered the prospect of liberation. It meant that there was no immaterial soul to survive death and thus no punishments or rewards to worry about in a hereafter. "Death is nothing to us" was the Epicurean watchword. To live fully in the moment surrounded by friends and like-minded loved ones provided a source of serenity and joy. Epicurus's school was nicknamed "The Garden" because that's where its adherents, both men and women, would gather—in Epicurus's backyard in Athens, a microcosm of Nature, whose workings they studied with delight.

Pleasure, Epicurus taught, is the alpha and omega of a happy life. But Epicurean pleasure was not wanton indulgence devoid of concern for the Earth or for others. It was a Middle Way, or Mean, as it were, between excess and defect. Indeed, Epicurean pleasure contained a good dose of frugality, even occasional asceticism. In pursuit of self-mastery, for example, Epicureans sometimes engaged in periods of fasting and even made a point to confess their shortcomings to one another, all with an eye to making progress in wholesome, carefree living. They even had a mantra to remind themselves of their core beliefs, the *tetrapharmakos*, or "four-fold remedy." Preserved among papyri discovered in the volcanic ash of Herculaneum, it reads, "God is nothing to be feared; death presents no worries; what is good is easy to obtain, and hardship easy to endure." An Epicurean in the time of the emperor Hadrian, Diogenes of Oenoanda (a city in what is now modern Turkey), felt so strongly about his convictions that he erected a billboard in stone, upon which were carved for all to see his philosophy's core doctrines. Given that it was grounded in a view of human beings as products of and active participants in the natural environment, Epicureanism begins to look like an ecological hedonism that we can live by still.

A key to its modern relevance is ancient Atomism's appeal to reasoned, empirical observation in support of its premises. While Lucretius's rich descriptions of natural phenomena tingle with emotion and shimmer with a sense of the sublime, his poem essentially comprises an argument, a demonstration, he believed, of scientific facts. And while the Epicureans' overarching purpose in embracing a materialist, scientific account of the world was to achieve personal equanimity and to pursue quietistic living, what they themselves called *ataraxia* ("unperturbedness"), it is a short journey from there to an active concern for the welfare of the Earth, our only home. Indeed, the Epicureans looked at being alive in this world with gratitude. "Thanks be to Blessed Nature," Epicurus writes, suffusing the *tetrapharmakos* with the language of benediction and a touch of paradox: "Because she has made what is necessary easy to obtain, and what it not easy to obtain unnecessary."

The Earth and its atmosphere, though it is an aggregate of myriad systems, is not an abstraction. As we experience it, it is the ground beneath our feet that feeds us and upon which we build our lives—and upon which, too, we inevitably have an impact. A revealing passage at the end of *De Rerum Natura* Book 2 indicates that Lucretius was aware of and worried about such impact—specifically, the depletion of the soil's fertility in his time—an issue that concerns the modern world even more so. Over just the past 150 years, modern humans have depleted half of the world's topsoil and, if things continue as they are going, we could run out of it completely in another 60. In arguing that natural growth, once it reaches its prescribed limit, will then fall to inevitable decline, Lucretius observes how "even today life is broken, and the Earth exhausted." Whereas the soil once burgeoned with living things of its own accord, it now produces only small yields of crops and livestock and even that, the poet says, is obtained with difficulty. The plowman shakes his head, bemoaning the present situation compared to times past. The vine dresser complains that previous generations cultivated less land, yet got higher yields, an outcome Lucretius attributes to Old World *pietas*—a word in Latin that means, not "piety" in the modern sense, but "duty," "obligation," and "scrupulous concern" toward objects of affection—in this case, the land. That Lucretius's report is not an idiosyncratic observation, or a contrived example to prove his point, but was a persistent issue for Roman farmers is indicated by the agronomist Columella, who, writing in the 60s CE, devotes his manual *De Re Rustica* to refuting what he says was the commonly held view that "the soil is now worn out and exhausted by overproduction in earlier days." The solution, Columella argues over the course of twelve books, is better farm management and the proper application of manure—a literal philosophy of compost.

We know next to nothing about Lucretius. That he composed the *De Rerum Natura* in the dying days of the Roman Republic, however, is significant. If, as seems likely, he was writing in the 50s BCE, those were volatile years of political uncertainty and unrest that culminated with Julius Caesar crossing the Rubicon in 49, after which the *mise-en-scène* at Rome was outright civil war. Lucretius may allude to that storm brewing

FIGURE 1.1. Sandro Botticelli (1445–1510), *Venus and Mars*.

in his opening invocation of Venus. Venus—for the atheistic Lucretius an avatar of Earth in that she is the source of all growth and reproduction—was also the mythological mother of Aeneas, Rome's founder, and thus of the Roman People. Lucretius beseeches Venus to lull to sleep her husband Mars, the god of war, as he languishes in her lap, so that her reign of peace might prevail.

Alma Venus—"Bountiful Venus"—are, in fact, the first two words of the poem, whereafter Lucretius's own *pietas* toward the venereal Earth animates every page. In this context it is telling that one of the several words for "atoms" in Lucretius's Latin, *materies*, derives from the word for "mother" (*mater*). Indeed, Lucretius is never far away from the sentiment expressed by the anonymous Homeric hymnist centuries before him who sings of Earth, the Mother of All: "To give life or to take it away rests with you." Or the Orphic hymnist after him, who praises Nature, whom he, too, calls "the Mother of All," thus: "You are everything! You alone fashion all things here."

Behold This Compost!

History tends to repeat itself, like the Russian folktales studied by Vladimir Propp (1895–1970). The attributes change but the forms and functions of events stay the same. Or perhaps it's more like Russian nesting dolls, with replica versions of the same forms and shapes encasing one another, only getting bigger. In nineteenth-century America another civil war impelled a different poet to muse along similar lines, and the parallels with Lucretius and the implications for living in the world today are striking.

Walt Whitman (1819–1892) first composed "This Compost!," a poem in *Leaves of Grass* eventually sandwiched between "Burial" and "I Hear America Singing," in 1856, five years before the onset of the American Civil War. "Something startles me where I thought I was safest," Whitman observes.

> I withdraw from the still woods I loved;
> I will not go now on the pastures to walk;
> I will not strip the clothes from my body to meet my
>   lover the sea;
> I will not touch my flesh to the earth, as to other flesh, to
>   renew me.
>
> O how can the ground not sicken?
> How can you be alive, you growths of spring?
> How can you furnish health, you blood of herbs, roots,
>   orchards, grain?
> Are they not continually putting distemper'd corpses in
>   you?
> Is not every continent work'd over and over with sour
>   dead?

Whitman's opening stanzas express trepidation and revulsion at the thought that the beautiful natural places he frequents might be infected by corpses of the "sour dead." "Where have you disposed of their carcasses?" he asks the Earth. "Those drunkards and gluttons of so many generations; / Where have you drawn off all the foul liquid and meat?" Whitman resolves to confirm his suspicion as follows—"I will run a furrow with my plough—I will press my spade through the sod, and turn it up underneath; / I am sure I shall expose some of the foul meat"— and yet is surprised and amazed to the contrary: "Behold this compost!" he declares. "Behold it well!"

> Perhaps every mite has once form'd part of a sick
>   person—Yet behold!
> The grass covers the prairies,
> The bean bursts noiselessly through the mould in the
>   garden,
> The delicate spear of the onion pierces upward,
> The apple-buds cluster together on the apple-branches,
> The resurrection of the wheat appears with pale visage
>   out of its graves,
> The tinge awakes over the willow-tree and the
>   mulberry-tree,
> The he-birds carol mornings and evenings, while the
>   she-birds sit on their nests,
> The young of poultry break through the hatch'd eggs,
> The new-born of animals appear—the calf is dropt from
>   the cow, the colt from the mare,
> Out of its little hill faithfully rise the potato's dark green
>   leaves,

> Out of its hill rises the yellow maize-stalk—the lilacs
>   bloom in the dooryards;
> The summer growth is innocent and disdainful above all
>   those strata of sour dead.

The phrase "resurrection of the wheat" in this stanza preserves the original title of the work ("Poem of Wonder at the Resurrection of the Wheat"), which Whitman changed to "This Compost!" for the 1867 edition of *Leaves of Grass*. In the 1871 edition he made an additional change by interpolating the phrase "the lilacs bloom in the dooryards," which evokes the title of his elegy to the assassinated president Abraham Lincoln and all the Civil War dead ("When Lilacs Last in the Dooryard Bloom'd"). The cross reference imparts a further dimension to the poem, making it a meditation on war and death as well as a celebration of Nature's resilience, not unlike Carl Sandburg's World War I poetic gem "Grass" a generation later. That theme and the amazement expressed at the Earth's power to create Life out of putrefaction are both markedly Lucretian. Whitman's focus on crops (beans, onions, apples, wheat, poultry, beef, potatoes, maize)—that is, growth as seen from the human vantage point of food—is particularly reminiscent of the *De Rerum Natura*. Compare this disquisition from Book 1:

> It must be admitted, then, that nothing can arise from nothing, since everything requires seed—the source wherefrom each created thing can be ushered into the air's gentle breezes. Also, since we see that lands that are farmed are superior to lands untended, and that they produce a better yield by the labor of human hands, it's quite clear that there are primordial elements of things in the ground that we activate

to fruition by turning over the fertile clods with the plough and by hoeing the ground-soil. If none of these things were so, you'd see crops grow much better of their own accord without our labor.

"Therefore, not a single thing returns to nothing," Lucretius concludes, harping on his ongoing refrain. "All things, rather, return by separation into the elemental bodies of matter." His peroration to clinch this point is so close to Whitman that one might be forgiven for thinking that Lucretius could well have been the poet's source:

Rain showers "pass away" when Father Ether has flung their drops into the lap of Mother Earth. Yet splendid crops spring up, and branches burgeon on trees, which become heavy themselves with fruit. From this source our human race and the animal kingdom are nourished in turn. From this source we see blessed cities abloom with children, and leafy forests resound everywhere with the songs of new birds. From this source, the herds, too, fat and weary, lay their bodies down in joyous pastures and the milky stream flows white from their swollen udders. From this source new lambs with feeble limbs play exuberantly on fresh pastures, their young brains drunk on straight milk. So, therefore, whatever you see does not wholly pass away, since Nature re-creates one thing from another and does not allow anything to be born except that fostered by the death of something else.

As Whitman watches the miracle of regeneration take place before his very eyes, he cries out "What chemistry!" That both air and water as well as Earth are "clean forever and forever" astounds him, as does the fact "that the cool drink from the well tastes so good," and

> That blackberries are so flavorous and juicy,
> That the fruits of the apple-orchard, and of the orange-
> orchard—
> that melons, grapes, peaches, plums, will none of them
> poison me,
> That when I recline on the grass I do not catch any
> disease,
> Though probably every spear of grass rises out of what
> was once a catching disease.

Whitman's apostrophe to the transformative power of chemistry in this, his penultimate stanza, betrays an intriguing clue that reveals the ultimate source for "This Compost!"'s themes. In 1847, when Whitman was in his late twenties and working as a newspaperman, he penned a short review of a newly published English-language edition of Justus von Liebig's *Chemistry in Its Application to Agriculture and Physiology* in the *Brooklyn Eagle*. "Chemistry!" Whitman writes there with telltale exclamation point, "the elevating, beautiful study! Chemistry—that involves the essence of creation, and the changes, and the growths, and formations and decays, of so large a constituent part of the earth, and the things thereof!"

Liebig (1803–1873) is considered one of the founders of organic chemistry and of biochemistry. He has also been dubbed the father of the modern fertilizer industry for his discovery of the critical roles played by nitrogen, phosphorus, potassium, and trace minerals in plant growth. Before Liebig's experiments and analyses, most chemists thought (like Lucretius) that humus, or decomposed organic matter, provided the source of nutrition for plants while the plants themselves, as living organisms, contributed some vital force of their own to activate the process of growth. Fertilizers like manure, it was believed, served primarily to break humus down, making it easier for plants to absorb the soil's goodness. Liebig, building on the work of his elder contemporary Karl Sprengel (1787–1859), disproved the humus theory by demonstrating that the chief value of humus and manure lay precisely in its inorganic mineral content. Typical humus, for example, was shown to contain on average 60 percent carbon, and smaller, but essential, proportions of nitrogen, phosphorus, and sulfur. "A time will come," Liebig predicted in 1840,

> when fields will be manured with a solution of glass (silicate of potash), with the ashes of burnt straw, and with the salts of phosphoric acid prepared in chemical manufactories, exactly as at present medicines are given for fever and goitre.

Though little more now than a footnote in the history of science, Liebig was a superstar in his day. His work did not need the admiring notice of a poetic newspaperman from Brooklyn, as he was already something of a household name, especially in Britain. The applications of Liebig's discoveries were far reaching. They extended, to put it in trendy modern idiom, from farm to fork: Not only did he develop recipes for synthetic fertilizers for application to farmers' fields, but also his forays into the chemistry of food transformed the products and procedures used in cooking. Liebig's research into the effects of extracting nutrients from solids like meat, and of concentrating substances like brewer's yeast, made possible the invention of British staples like Oxo brand bouillon, for example, which hit the shelves in 1900, and Marmite, which debuted in 1902.

The advent of Liebig's agricultural chemistry dovetailed perfectly with the predicaments and aspirations of mid-nineteenth-century Europe. Britain, for example, was already busy reaping benefits from its so-called Second Agricultural Revolution. New practices in farming (crop rotations involving turnips and clover, the wheel-less plow); land management (conversion of forestland to arable ground and pasture, reclamation and drainage of wetlands); and new arrangements in tenancy (the Enclosure Movement) had been achieving greater efficiencies and higher crop yields for decades prior. The repeal of the price-protectionist Corn Laws in 1846, however—brought on by the prohibitively high cost of bread for a growing population—soon flooded the market with cheap, imported grain, leaving British farmers scrambling to find even greater efficiencies to compete. The fallout thrust Liebig further into the spotlight. However, as the industrialization of Europe's economy began to impose its grislier effects on the urban poor, and as he learned more about methods in what came to known as British High Farming, Liebig became increasingly concerned about soil—and social—health, his tone urgent and polemical. By the time he issued the seventh edition of *Agricultural Chemistry* in 1862, Liebig was decrying the "robbery system" (*Raubsystem*) of contemporary agriculture in terms like these:

Great Britain deprives all countries of the conditions of their fertility. It has raked up the battle-fields of Leipsic, Waterloo, and the Crimea; it has consumed the bones of many generations accumulated in the catacombs of Sicily; and now annually destroys the food for a future generation of three millions and a half of people. Like a vampire it hangs on the breast of Europe, and even the world, sucking its life-blood.

In addition to scouring the Continent's battlefields and graveyards for human bones to grind up into meal for fertilizer—one can imagine what Whitman would have made of that—Britain was importing millions of tons of guano from Peru, all of it harvested and transported under appalling conditions by Chinese work gangs. Liebig's indictment of this situation caught the attention of his contemporary and fellow German, Karl Marx, who was by then living in London. Marx, too, denounced the "robbery-system" of Victorian agriculture and would employ Liebig's vampire imagery to depict the whole of the market economy, characterizing capital as "dead labor" that "vampire-like" preys upon its victims "by sucking living labor." The problem, Marx and Engels went on to argue later in the third volume of *Capital* (1894), is that "the entire spirit of capitalist production is oriented toward the most immediate monetary profit [and] stands in contradiction to agriculture, which has to concern itself with the whole gamut of permanent conditions of life required by the chain of human generations." In Marx's analysis, the harmful agricultural practices that Liebig had identified inevitably lead to "an irreparable rift in the interdependent process of social metabolism, a metabolism prescribed by the natural laws of life itself." But if Marxism, with the benefit of hindsight, has proved to be problematic in practice, one can just as readily lend an ear to a Scots poet-farmer, who was singing the same tune a century before Marx in the heady, early days of High Farming in Britain. Robert Burns's poetic apology *To a Mouse, on Turning Her Up in Her Nest with the Plough, November 1785,* for example, makes the same observation with only slightly different emphasis:

I'm truly sorry Man's dominion
Has broken Nature's social union,
An' justifies that ill opinion,
    Which makes thee startle,
At me, thy poor, earth-born companion,
    An' *fellow-mortal*!

In using the word metabolism, ancient Greek for "change," or "exchange," to describe the law-like interdependence of Nature and human society, Marx was borrowing a term from the domain of Liebig and his scientific colleagues. Metabolism describes the chemical reactions that take place in organisms to convert the energy found in food to energy usable by other organisms. Similar chemical reactions also govern organisms' ability to digest and eliminate metabolic wastes. The whole process is reciprocal and regenerative. Liebig called it *Stoffwechsel* ("elemental exchange") and was adamant that the chemistry of soil requires giving back to the Earth. "A field from which something is permanently taken away cannot possibly increase or even continue equal in productive power," he argued. "The axiom thus enunciated," Liebig insisted further, "is simply a natural law." In so saying, he was echoing the Lucretian principle as reformulated by Lavoisier in *Traité élémentaire de chimie* (1789), the world's first chemistry textbook, that, in Nature, "nothing is lost; nothing is created; everything is transformed."

While Marx clearly followed Liebig's science on matters of soil, he also derives his ideas, as so much of his materialist worldview, from Lucretius and ancient Atomism. His PhD dissertation from 1841, for example, probed the differences between the atomistic philosophies of Democritus and Epicurus, for which Lucretius provides a main source of evidence. In speaking of "an irreparable rift" between social and natural processes caused by a capitalist economy, Marx echoes the Epicurean distinction between innate properties that attach to things naturally ("weight to stone, heat to fire, liquidity to water, touch to all bodies, intangibility to empty space," as Lucretius puts it) and mere accidental properties that "come and go while the nature of things remains intact," to wit: "slavery, poverty and riches; freedom, war and peace." As Marx himself states in *The Poverty of Philosophy* (1847), his broadside against the anarchist Proudhon, such concepts "are as little eternal as the relations they express. They are *historical and transitory*," conditioned by prevailing social and economic forces. By contrast, he continues, alluding to another passage from Lucretius, "the only immutable thing is *mors immortalis* (Death the Immortal)," toward which all growth inclines and, inevitably, culminates.

Marx's appeal to the metabolisms of Nature as the yardstick for measuring human social relations and his concern for quality of life in the here and now in the shadow of Immortal Death puts him squarely in Lucretius's camp. What one modern scholar says in summary of Marx's thinking on these matters is equally true of Lucretius: "His entire dialectical framework rested on what would today be called an ecological (or socioecological) systems theory, connecting the materialist conception of history to that of nature." Marx's collaborator and protégé Friedrich Engels harps on the centrality of systemic relationships again and again in his multilingual mélange of notes about then recent developments in natural science, published posthumously in 1925 as *Dialectics of Nature*. "In nature," he writes, "nothing takes place in isolation. Everything affects every other thing and *vice versa*." In articulating what he called the "law of the transformation of quantity into quality" in natural systems, Engels anticipated what we now call *emergence*, that a whole is other than the sum of its parts. The point was foreshadowed by Aristotle, but its scientific demonstration was made by a chemist, as it happens, Ilya Prigogine, for which he won the Nobel Prize in 1977. Theoretical physicist P. W. Anderson, skirting the edges of the concept, employed a marvelous tag to describe this pervasive feature in Nature: "More Is Different," the title of his own groundbreaking essay in *Science* from 1972. "More is different" and the "transformation of quantity into quality," however, is no source for optimism, solace, or blind hope. It serves rather as a warning since emergent properties in Nature and social systems alike cannot always be anticipated and are often destructive because exponential in scale of growth or complexity. What begins as a snowflake ends in an avalanche. Simple patterns of ones and zeros produce abominations like the computer HAL in *2001: A Space Odyssey*, ChatGPT, or so-called deepfakes. "Less is more," as we shall see shortly, is an apt phrase for the appropriate human response.

Marx and Engels, of course, were revolutionaries. Lucretius and other followers of Epicureanism were quietists. But to take Nature seriously, whatever your political views or temperamental stripe, to try to align transitory, historically conditioned values, social arrangements, and institutions with first principles in Nature is, at this point in our history with the Earth, our only option for survival. In fact, to analogize from another item in the long list of Liebig's discoveries, to follow Nature's lead in this way could ultimately be a source for flourishing—if we abide by it.

The Law of the Minimum

It might seem surprising, given today's world of mass-produced, commodified food, that the most enduring of Liebig's legacies is not Marx, or Marmite, or chemical fertilizers, but the articulation of a feature of plant growth that finds expression in the whole of Nature. One might call it the Goldilocks Principle. Liebig, from his vantage point as a chemist, called it the Law of the Minimum.

In at least one version of the Story of the Three Bears, Goldilocks tastes three bowls of porridge, finding one too hot, one too cold, but the third "just right." Liebig discovered similarly that the conditions for optimal growth in plants need to be "just right"—specifically, that the rate and quality of growth is determined not by the total amount of nutrients available in the soil and atmosphere but is limited by the scarcest necessary element. In the case of plants and trees, Liebig's Law is typically illustrated by the image of a barrel consisting of unequal staves, which represent nutrient inputs. Among the eighteen nutrients that contribute to plant growth, three are predominant and essential to productive soil: nitrogen, phosphorus, and potassium, which correspond to the "NPK numbers" you'll see on bags of fertilizer—Pro-Gro brand, for example, an organic general fertilizer, where 5-3-4 means 5 percent nitrogen ("N" in the periodic table), 3 percent phosphate ($\approx$ phosphorus, "P"), and 4 percent potash ($\approx$ potassium, "K").

The barrel in this analogy can only be as full as the shortest stave, which represents the element present in the smallest quantity. The yield or quality of growth of a particular plant is inhibited by the least available resource. Conversely, excessive

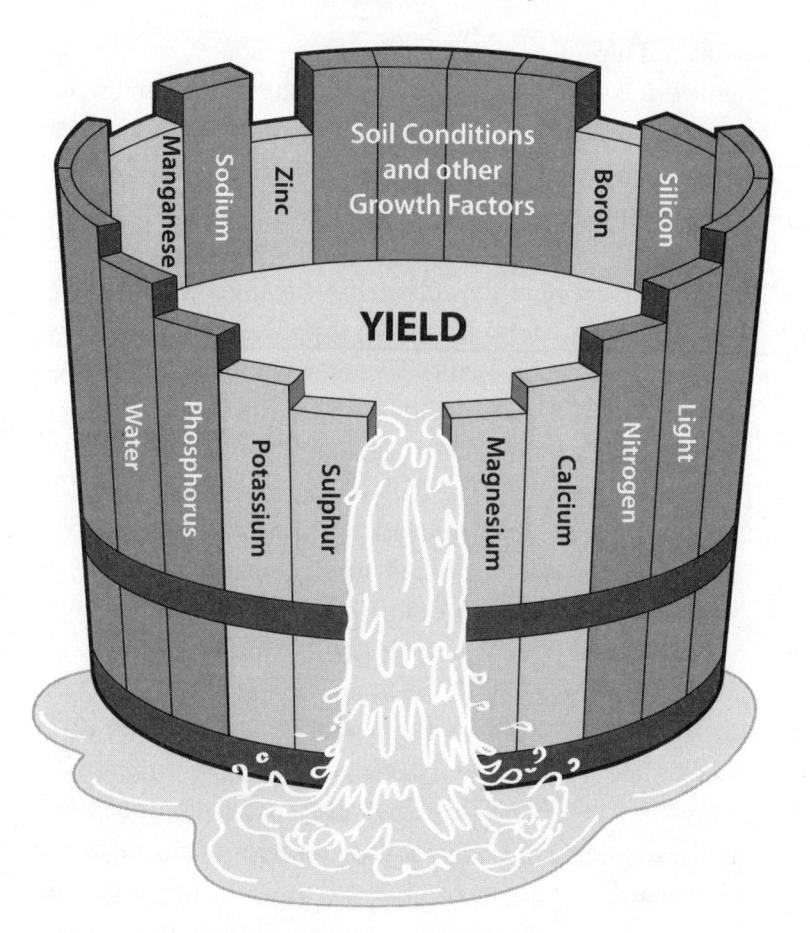

FIGURE 1.2. Liebig's Barrel.

amounts of elements can produce undesirable results. On our farm, we feed large round bales of hay to our sheep out on frozen, snowy pasture in winter. When the ground has thawed in spring, the first thing to crop up where the bales were positioned while the sheep ate them, scattering, as they do, inedible stalks and tiny seeds and manuring the perimeter, are stinging nettles. This is because the hay-pack is super-rich in nitrogen from the fresh manure and from moisture retained in the thick layer of compacted hay, conditions on which nettles thrive. The patches of nettle-bloom that dot the otherwise glorious landscape look like alien crop circles—a delight for the eyes, perhaps, when seen from above, but a bane for the shepherd on the ground, as sheep don't eat nettles. If you let them go to seed, you'll have even more nettles the following year and will soon be left with a field of weeds, not a pasture. There's a reason they say that if you raise livestock, what you really are is a grass farmer.

The year 2022 marked the fiftieth anniversary of the book *The Limits to Growth*. That landmark indictment of human overreach and excess, first published in 1972 and updated every five years since, is a bible of the environmental movement. In our new climatic regime of global heating, it remains scripture still, even if it is not infallible on the finer detail. The book's authors, the late Donella Meadows and her fellow researchers at MIT via the Club of Rome, used systems modeling to demonstrate that while rates of increase in the world's population, pollution levels, and depletion of natural resources are fundamentally exponential in nature, our capacity to remediate these problems is confined to a linear trajectory. Instead of progress, the argument insists, we need regress; in lieu of growth, degrowth.

The Law of the Minimum is one of Nature's givens. It can't be undone, only deployed to one's advantage or ignored to one's detriment. We cannot countermand it with technology by substituting artificial, synthetic substances or catalysts for natural ones since technology itself is ultimately subject to Liebig limits (the availability of natural resources and energy). Phosphorus, at any rate, is an element that cannot be synthesized, and its reserves are finite. But the contemporary problem is bigger, and worse. Feeding the world's 8 billion people requires us to produce hundreds of millions of tons of ammonia each year, whose chemical synthesis forms the basis of all nitrogen fertilizers. The irony here is thick, as it was Liebig's research that led to the use of inorganic compounds in agriculture. Yet the application of that research runs up against the kind of natural limits that Liebig championed. The mass production of ammonia relies heavily on the combustion of fossil fuels. Synthetic fertilizers used to produce food on a mass scale are thus dependent on the extraction of nonrenewable resources, making them a major source of greenhouse gas emissions even before they enter the ground and begin contributing to the downward spiral of depleting the soil's fertility. The whole situation is a classic, compounded instance of a Jevons Paradox, wherein a technological innovation that improves efficiency or effectiveness only increases demand and externalized costs. It is no accident that Jevons, a Victorian-era economist, was a contemporary of Liebig, and came to his discovery by way of another incipient "robbery-system" at Nature's expense—coal—where an improvement to the design of the steam engine by James Watt (1736–1819) made the pumping of water from coal mines more efficient, leading to more cost-effective production and utilization of coal, which in turn contributed to its increased and more widespread use. It made the Industrial Revolution possible, and Blake's dark Satanic Mills inevitable. As Jevons summarizes his argument in *The Coal Question* (1865), "It is a confusion of ideas to suppose that the economical use of fuel is equivalent to diminished consumption. The very contrary is the truth."

The ethical corollary to Liebig's Law is as old as philosophy itself. At Apollo's Oracle at Delphi, two phrases were inscribed at the entrance to the temple: "Nothing in Excess" and "Know Thyself." Both are traditional pieces of folk wisdom that speak to the need to live within socioecological bounds, and are made from the same notional stock as Greek myths—that of Actaeon, for example, a hunter who intrudes upon Artemis, an Earth goddess, in her sacred grove and is punished by being torn apart by his own dogs; or Erysichthon, who chops down an oak tree sacred to Demeter, another avatar of Earth, and is afflicted with perpetual hunger, forced to prostitute his daughter in exchange for food, and, ultimately, to cannibalize his own body in order to survive. The maxims of Delphi eventually became philosophical catchphrases with existential and ethical coloring. Aristotle, for example, argues in the *Nicomachean Ethics* that virtue clings to a Mean between excess and defect. The tragedian Sophocles dishes up an object lesson about self-knowledge in the *Oedipus Rex*, as does Euripides in his *Bacchae*. Several centuries after Sophocles, Euripides, and Aristotle, the Neoplatonist philosopher Plotinus pays homage to the wisdom of both Delphic imperatives in his essay "On Beauty," the image he draws from sculpture perfectly and appropriately Apolline:

> Withdraw into yourself and look. And if you do not find yourself beautiful yet, act as does the creator of a statue that is to be made beautiful: he cuts away here, he smooths there, he makes this line lighter, this other purer, until a lovely face has grown upon his work. So do you also: cut away all that is excessive, straighten all that is crooked, bring light to all that is overcast, labour to make all one glow of beauty and never

cease chiseling your statue, until there shall shine out on you from it the godlike splendour of virtue, until you shall see the perfect goodness surely established in the stainless shrine.

Creation and growth by subtraction—to "cut away all that is excessive"—is an ethos and aesthetic whose time has come. In horticultural terms, prune a plant back hard and it will come back to be even more vigorous and healthy. Less rich soil often produces better flowers. On the last of 513 dizzying pages of statistics and technical detail in his monumental book *Growth: From Microorganisms to Megacities* (2019), Vaclav Smil concludes by giving the Roman poet Horace the final word on human societies' dire need for limits to growth: "There is a mean in things," Horace observes. "Ultimately, there are fixed limits on either side of which what is right cannot exist." That verdict, which Smil reaches though exhaustive analysis, derives from Aristotle via Delphi, though Horace himself, as readers of his poetry have readily surmised, was also sympathetic to Epicurean views, even if he was not a card-carrying member of the school. Indeed, the notion that there are limits in Nature that we cannot and must not exceed is arguably *the* characteristic feature of all ancient thinking. Lucretius himself repeatedly calls this condition of things a "pact" or "treaty" with Nature, arguing from what he believed to be atomic fact that "there is a limit to growth and of preserving Life to things according to kind"; that "it is solemnly decreed by the treaties of Nature what each kind of thing can and cannot do." As with territorial boundaries drawn between nations and the laws that govern international relations in the human realm, it is incumbent on us to respect the compacts of Nature.

Humility

"Now I am terrified at the earth!" Whitman exudes in his closing stanza of "This Compost!"

> It is that calm and patient,
> It grows such sweet things out of such corruptions,
> It turns harmless and stainless on its axis, with such
>   endless successions of diseas'd corpses,
> It distils such exquisite winds out of such infused fetor,
> It renews with such unwitting looks, its prodigal, annual,
>   sumptuous crops,
> It gives such divine materials to men, and accepts such
>   leavings from them at last.

If he was merely alluding before, Whitman is practically channeling Lucretius now. The last line is virtually a paraphrase of the Epicurean tenet that nothing comes from nothing or returns to nothing. Indeed, it's a recurrent theme in *Leaves of Grass*. "The smallest sprout shows there is really no death," Whitman croons in "Song of Myself." "All goes onward and outward, nothing collapses, / And to die is different from what any one supposed, and luckier." That a prodigal Earth gives us divine materials and accepts our leavings at last also recalls the sentiments we've seen expressed in the Homeric Hymn to Earth ("To give life and to take it rests with you"). The terror that Whitman feels when confronted with the awesome, transformative power of the Earth is also wholly Lucretian: Lucretius is likewise filled with "preternatural delight, and a shudder" when he contemplates the extravagant processes of regeneration in Nature. It is no wonder that Jane Bennett, a proponent of the so-called New Materialist school of contemporary thought, sees in both Lucretius and Whitman support for the New Materialists' view that matter and objects possess an agentive, vibrant, interactive force that shapes our physical and social worlds. In a universe where mass is equivalent to energy, as modern physics instructs, that conclusion is perhaps not so surprising. And yet the New Materialists' dynamic image of the universe and of Earth, whatever else it might be, is not in fact new. It goes back further even than Lucretius or Whitman, and deeper.

The Oracle at Delphi, with its complex of ancient shrines, sacred sites, and slogans, will be familiar to most readers and modern visitors to Greece as the possession of the god Apollo. It was not always so. Apollo, the old stories say, wrested Delphi from Earth (Gaia) and the Oracle's protecting serpent Pytho by force, effecting a mythological ascendency of male rulers over female, chthonic powers. In the account of Creation by Hesiod (a farmer-poet, like Burns, from the eighth century BCE) Gaia, or Earth, produces her own consort Ouranous ("Sky") by parthenogenesis. Ouranos is soon supplanted, however, by his son Cronos, who is in turn overthrown by his son, Zeus—in both instances, paradoxically, with assistance from their respective mothers. Ancient visitors to Delphi would have been shown the "navel" of the world, as was the Greek travel writer and antiquarian Pausanias in the second century CE. The spot was marked by what was touted as the very stone coughed up by Cronos in the ruse devised by Zeus's mother Rhea, as related in Hesiod's tale. (Cronos had swallowed all his children as soon as they were born to prevent dynastic succession but was fooled by a stone substituted for his youngest child, Zeus, who later dethroned him.) Navels, of course, were once umbilicals—which makes Delphi something of a womb of Earth, from whose crevices arose, according to some ancient accounts, a vaporous steam that inspired Apollo's seer-priestess, the Pythia (named after the vanquished serpent), to issue oracular pronouncements that were deemed binding for both the individuals and states that consulted her.

Bruno Latour rehearses these accounts in his book *Facing Gaia* (2017). He, too, like Whitman, is terrified of the Earth. Latour finds Hesiod's Gaia "dangerous," "somber," "savvy," even "monstrous." "What is certain is that she is not a figure of harmony," he writes, and "there is nothing maternal about her." The Gaia that ultimately concerns him, however, is not Hesiod's, nor Delphi's original proprietary deity, but James Lovelock and Lynn Margulis's scientific model of a self-regulating biosphere—the living superorganism that Lovelock dubbed "Gaia," our dynamical planet Earth. Despite its unscientific associations with a mythological deity, Gaia is a term and concept Latour finds more apt for describing the interacting processes of our new climatic regime than, say, "The Anthropocene," which reinforces a dangerously false distinction, he thinks, between humans and the nonhuman world. He eschews, too, the very word "Nature." For Latour, Gaia is preferable because it is, paradoxically, "wholly secular" and "*much less* a religious figure than Nature is." He explains what he means in a flourish of statements that, like the *obiter dicta* of the Pythia at Delphi, are cast in an oracular mode: "The climate is the historical result of reciprocal connections." "Gaia is a *power of historicization.*" "Gaia

FIGURE 1.3. Gnōthi Sauton ("Know Thyself"), Baths of Diocletian, Rome, ca. first century CE.

is *an injunction to rematerialize our belonging to the world.*" "In the face of what is to come, we cannot continue to believe in the old future if we want to have a future at all. This is what I mean by 'facing Gaia.'"

My own point in marshaling the likes of Lucretius, Liebig, Whitman, and Marx to underscore the need to totalize our engagement with the Earth—scientifically, ethically, affectively—corresponds to yet another ancient word and concept: *humility*, from Latin *humus*, meaning "the quality or condition of being close to the ground." In other words, *facing Gaia*. The alternative posture is conveyed by that other Delphic injunction—not "Nothing in Excess," because if we fail in humility, it will be too late for that. But "Know Thyself," as depicted on a tessellated

Roman mosaic from the once opulent, now dilapidated, Baths of Diocletian. The image is of a skeletal corpse, reclining in repose and destined for decay.

———

Of course, everything dies in the end. To philosophize, Socrates declared on his own deathbed, is to rehearse for this inevitable result. When Epicurus died, he deposited his will in the public archive at Athens—the Metroön, a shrine dedicated to the Mother of the Gods located at the city's civic heart, the Agora. The temple contained a magnificent statue, sculpted by a student of Phidias, the Michelangelo of Athens. It depicted the Great Mother, seated, holding a tambourine, and flanked by lions. It's an image as old as civilization itself: the Neolithic "Mistress of the Animals" who presided over the powers of Nature, images of whom have been discovered in the earliest cities and towns.

The Metroön stood adjacent to the Old Bouleuterion, Athens's first council chamber, the foundational institution of the world's first democracy, established in 508 BCE. Steles with written laws were erected in front of the Metroön for public viewing. Court documents were filed there for safekeeping. The Great Mother, an avatar of Earth, as we have seen, was for the Athenians not only the goddess of Nature, but a guarantor of justice in the social sphere as well. The poet Solon (ca. 630–560 BCE), Athens's archetypal lawgiver, makes the connection explicit in describing his reformist program of debt cancellation and redistribution of land in the sixth century BCE: "She better than any other can give witness in the court of time, the very great Mother of the Olympian gods, black Earth." Lucretius's opening paean to bountiful

FIGURE 1.4. "Mistress of the Animals," Çatalhöyük, Turkey, ca. 6000 BCE.

Venus evokes these ancient associations in a Roman setting. For our own age, philosopher Michel Serres, like Bennett a great admirer of Lucretius, calls on humanity to reaffirm its ancient compacts with Nature in his prose poem *The Natural Contract* (1990). In tone and orientation, Serres's ode to Earth in the book's concluding pages sounds like it could have been composed by the author of the Orphic Hymn to Nature:

> Mother . . . faithful mother . . . solitary for as long as the world has existed, the heaviest, the most fecund, the holiest of maternal dwellings, chaste because always alone, and always pregnant, virgin and mother of all living things, better than alive, irreproducible universal womb of all possible life, mirror of ice floes, seat of snows, vessel of the seas, rose of the winds, tower of ivory, house of gold, Ark of the Covenant, gate of heaven, health, refuge, queen surrounded by clouds.
>
> Who will be able to move her, who will be able to take her in their arms, who will protect her when she risks dying and when she begins her mortal agony?

The terms of Epicurus's will aimed to ensure the continuation of the Garden, his school, and the Epicureans' shared way of life. It is a remarkable document that gives us a glimpse into the duty of care practiced in the inner circle, and the seriousness of their collective endeavor. Epicurean philosophy flourished for nearly three centuries in the Greek East afterward. It made inroads to Rome when Philodemus (110–30 BCE), a native of Gadara (a Hellenistic city in modern Jordan), moved to Campania from Athens and became a prominent proponent. Philodemus, a poet and philosopher, the teacher of Vergil, was Lucretius's contemporary. A large library containing many of his previously unknown writings continues to be unearthed at Herculaneum in the so-called Villa of the Papyri, which was destroyed, but well preserved in volcanic ash, along with Pompeii, by the eruption of Vesuvius in 79 CE. Philodemus's work shows an Epicureanism that was still orthodox in its core doctrines, yet responsive to the cultural milieu of its time. In the following three centuries of the Common Era, the rise of Christianity and a revival of Platonism as the dominant mode of thought thrust Epicureanism into relative obscurity, until it blossomed again in the early Renaissance with the discovery of a sole manuscript of the *De Rerum Natura*—a work thought to have been lost at the time—by Poggio in 1417. Since then, there have been reams of scholarship on Lucretius and Epicureanism, and at least one popular, Pulitzer Prize–winning book.

Can one practice Epicureanism today? And, if so, how, and to what end? To the extent that everyone with a rudimentary education now understands that all matter in the universe consists of atoms and their combinations into molecules, we are all Epicureans. It's the ethical imperative to live and make decisions as if that were true that we've lost and would do well to recover. To live as if scientific facts were actionable, as if your happiness depended on them, to live simply and circumspectly in the present yet to take the long view—that is the legacy of Epicurus. One other thing is crystal clear from the Epicurean way of life: Reverence, wonder, and awe are not incompatible with a scientific, even atheistic, understanding of a world in which the only certainty is death. Lucretius and his epigone Whitman show that such a response is rational, and in keeping with knowledge of the facts. In *Learning to Die in the Anthropocene* (2015), Roy Scranton stumbles afresh upon this ancient realization.

"Our knowledge of this vast universe remains ridiculously limited," he writes.

At the same time, that same knowledge is utterly awesome. For a growth of carbon scum on a spinning rock in the backwater of an unremarkable galaxy light years from anywhere to develop the technology to send radio telescopes into space to measure the age of the universe is a prodigious achievement. Our primate curiosity and intellectual hubris have inspired breathtaking audacities. Just a few thousand years ago, we were learning to make marks on clay. In the blink of an eye we've brushed our fingers against eternity.

Scranton sounds an awful lot here like an ancient Greek— less Epicurus than Sophocles, who similarly marveled at our species' capacity for technological feats and worried about their environmental impact. "Human cleverness," Sophocles observes through the Chorus in the *Antigone*, "exceeding all expectations, wears away the highest of the gods, the unwearying, unwithering Earth, as the horse-driven plow furrows back and forth, year after year, turning the soil"—to which Liebig or Marx might add "exhausting it."

Ancient ways of living in a dying world like Epicureanism give a glimmer of hope that all is not lost or yet exhausted, that we've been down this road before, and that there is wisdom still to be resurrected and renewed. Older modes of thinking and imagining also serve as a reminder that, in sourcing solutions to the climate and other human catastrophes, "the fate of the humanities," as Scranton himself concludes, "is the fate of humanity itself."

2

"There Are Gods Here Too"

IN AN INFLUENTIAL and widely read essay titled "Why Look at Animals?" art critic and novelist John Berger decries the alienation that sets in between human and nonhuman species in a capitalist economy. The alienation Berger describes manifests itself in many ways in modern societies but perhaps most conspicuously in the anthropomorphizing of animals as pets and the objectification of them in zoos. Of course, humans were anthropomorphizing animals (and making theriomorphs of themselves) long before the dawn of capitalism, as Berger himself duly notes. The epithets of Homeric poetry ("owl-eyed Athena," "lion-hearted Achilles"), the fables of Aesop, or the Buddhist *Jataka Tales*, to say nothing of Amerindian and Aboriginal totemism, make that perfectly clear. But, according to Berger, these ancient expressions were gestures of interspecies proximity and affinity, not the frivolous, jaded compensations for alienation that they have become. It was only in the thrall of money—a power and means of exchange dissociated from the biological processes of life—that humans began to see themselves as separate from Nature and superior to it. This ushered in a new noetic and sociocultural dispensation that made possible not only zoos but also factory farms, disregard for the integrity of habitats, and all the attendant repercussions that such careless attitudes and actions entail, like deforestation, overfishing, species extinction, and loss of biodiversity.

Parts and Wholes, of Animals

The scientific study of animals follows in the wake of this historical development. It, too, is a form of objectification, one likewise fraught with potentially perilous outcomes. And yet, the example and evidence that animals themselves provide is also ripe with possibility for a return to ecological living. Aristotle, the world's first scientific biologist, had some remarkable things to say toward that end. Why look at animals? Berger is eloquent, but lends himself to paraphrase. Aristotle's answer to that question, from his treatise *Parts of Animals*, written around 350 BCE, deserves to be experienced verbatim:

> We assert that there two sorts of beings in Nature, those that are without origin, eternal, and indestructible, and those that participate in processes of birth and decay. It follows that those beings in the first category, although precious because divine, are less susceptible to investigation because there is scant empirical evidence for what we yearn to know about them. But concerning beings that perish, like plants and animals, we are better provided for in gaining knowledge because we live alongside them. Indeed, anyone who cares enough to put in the work can discover a great deal about

each of their various kinds. Nonetheless, both sorts of beings have their own charm.

So, while it's clear that our grasp of eternal subjects is slight, nonetheless, because they are precious, knowledge of them is more delightful than knowledge of everything else that falls in our orbit, just as it is more delightful to get a partial, fleeting glimpse of those we love than to review a host of quotidian details with precision, even if those, too, are important. Subjects of study on Earth, on the other hand, because we have more and better information about them, take priority when it comes to knowledge because they are nearer to us and more akin to our nature. Such pursuits compensate somewhat for the philosophy that concerns itself with theology.

So, now that we have rehearsed and presented our views on theological subjects, it remains to speak about animals and their nature. To the extent that we can, we will leave no animal out, whether it be regarded as valueless or highly prized. For even in dealing with animals that are less pleasing to the senses, when a person of natural philosophic bent considers them from a scientific point of view, someone who can understand the causes of things, Nature, in displaying its handiwork, presents pleasures beyond compare. . . . Therefore, we must not flinch, as if we were children, at the careful consideration of less-esteemed animals, for in all of Nature there is something wonderful.

There is a story that some strangers from out of town once came to visit the philosopher Heraclitus, and when they found him warming himself by the bread oven, they stopped short at the door. Whereupon Heraclitus said, "Take heart!

Come on in! For there are gods here, too!" Just so, we, too, ought to undertake research about every kind of animal with no fear or squeamishness since all of them contain Nature and possess Beauty. I add "Beauty" because it is purpose and not chance that is most at work in Nature, and the purpose for which animals have been formed or the end for which they have been created takes its place among what counts as beautiful.

If, however, someone has concluded that the study of animals is an undistinguished pursuit, on that same logic he ought to think the same about the study of himself. For it's impossible to look upon the components from which a human being is constructed—blood, flesh, bones, veins, and so on—without a good deal of disgust. Relatedly, we should understand that someone who discusses any of these individual parts and their arrangements is not describing their material composition for its own sake but is concerned rather with the conformation of a whole. The same is true of a house—it's the whole structure that matters, not the bricks, mortar, and timber. Likewise, too, in Nature: the objective is to describe the synthetic whole, not the individual parts that do not occur separately apart from their combination as an entity.

To say that there's much here to unpack would be an understatement, yet also the wrong way to put it, as Aristotle's remarks are so admirably clear. Somehow, in only a few paragraphs, he manages to present the best case perhaps ever made for the inherent worth of both physical and metaphysical pursuits. Objects of pure thought, existential reality, divine beings, which for Aristotle include not only God, gods, and goddesses, but stars and planets, too, are all difficult to know. Nonetheless, to pursue knowledge of such things provides the deepest source of joy and comprises the highest form of human longing and aspiration. Even a fleeting glimpse of those we love, as he puts it, is more satisfying than intimate knowledge of an encyclopedia of facts.

We are on surer footing, however, in studying the physical, natural world. Animals are especially useful in this regard since "they are nearer to us and more akin to our nature." We should therefore pursue zoology and biology, Aristotle insists, with eagerness and confidence. Here it is instructive perhaps to recall the origin of the word "metaphysics," the title of another major work by Aristotle, which was so called for its placement by an ancient editor of Aristotle's *oeuvre after* (Greek *meta*) his treatises concerning physics. Metaphysics thus means simply "after the *Physics.*" The etymology of the word "physics" is similarly revealing, as its original meaning encompasses much more than it does today. Derived from the Greek verb *phuō* ("to grow"), it refers to investigative research into all of Nature, or, as Aristotle puts it earlier, of objects that "participate in processes of birth and decay." Metaphysics, then, looking at both the development of the word itself and the value assigned to it by Aristotle, might best be viewed as the precious afterthought we entertain while engrossed in studying the natural world.

The use of the humble preposition *meta* to describe subjects of study beyond the compass of the terrestrial sphere has grown out of all proportion to become today a shorthand term for anything that is excessively or exclusively self-referential. Metadiscourse—talk about talk—comes to mind, but so does the parent company formerly known as Facebook, which promises to open new vistas onto a simulated multiverse of virtual everything. In contrast, however, to Meta and its involuted, self-absorbed "Metaverse," Aristotle exhorts us to practice old-fashioned empiricism in the world of sensible objects. To study animals, Aristotle suggests, is to hold up a mirror to ourselves. Even small or repellent creatures—leeches, say, or maggots—should compel our attention, as the causes and purposes of their morphology and behavior contribute to a better understanding of ourselves. People, after all, are animals, too. One can only imagine the field day Aristotle would have had with DNA. As is well known now, but was wholly unknown then, 99 percent of our genetic information is shared with chimpanzees. We have about 90 percent in common with mice; 65 percent with chickens, which are not even mammals; 60 percent with bananas, which are not even animals. It is hardly trite or a truism to insist that all living things are connected.

Aristotle's insistence at the end of this passage from *Parts of Animals* that scientific investigation should always be concerned with systemic wholes is thus particularly inspired. Proponents of modern complexity science tend to present systems research in grandiose terms. In the words of one practitioner, systems science represents "a scientific revolution," "the forefront of a new discipline." Aristotle's own two-thousand-year-old image is simpler, more down to earth, and, ironically, more holistic—the construction of a house, where bricks, mortar, and timber contribute to a whole that does not exist or function separately from its parts. "House," we have seen, lies at the very heart of "ecology."

Not everyone, thank God, practices an academic discipline. We all, however, need somewhere to live. Writ large, the Earth is that ultimate home. Visionary designer and craftsman William Morris (1834–1896) once famously declared "Have nothing in your houses that you do not know to be useful or think to be beautiful." Aristotle says that such is already the case in Nature: whatever pertains to ecology also possesses beauty. This is so, he says, because purpose, not chance, characterizes the arrangement of parts in the world. As Aristotle sums up this point elsewhere, "Nature does nothing in vain." In a variation on that same theme, he approaches Morris's advice: "In Nature there is nothing superfluous." Thrifty on the one hand (think of a thousand-pound cow thriving on a few acres of pasture), extravagant on the other (consider the male peacock's eye-popping plumage), Nature nonetheless provides exactly the right conditions for life. It falls to us to understand and act on those conditions. The cow, for example, efficiently converts a food source inedible to humans (grass) into usable energy and useful by-products; the peacock relies on its display to attract a mate and reproduce itself. In all of Nature, Aristotle observes, there is something wonderful.

Parts and Wholes, of Everything

Aristotle's passing remark about the philosopher Heraclitus (ca. 535–475 BCE) is more than just an anecdote to enliven his treatise. It conveys a key concept about the relationship of parts to systemic whole, of micro- to macrocosm, and thus, ultimately, of organisms, including humans, to the rest of Nature. Visitors come from afar to consult the sage of Ephesus as if he were an oracle. They are surprised, however, to find the great one huddled up, warming himself by a lowly bread oven in the kitchen. Heraclitus, a cryptic, paradoxical thinker, and probably, too, a guru-like personality, believed that fire, owing to its dynamic changeability and transformative power, was a visible image of the stuff of which the universe is composed. Today we would call that energy, or the interplay of atomic particles. For Heraclitus,

> This universe, the same for all, was not made by gods or humans. Rather, it always was and is and shall be—an everlasting fire, kindling itself in measures and extinguishing itself in measures.

In another of his Zen-like fragments he puts the matter this way: "All things are an exchange for fire and fire for all things, as gold is for goods and goods for gold." The first statement, with its twice-repeated phrase "in measures," suggests that cosmic processes involve self-regulation and proportional calibration. The second, with its reference to economic exchange, analogizes not only visible fire to those invisible cosmic processes, but Nature to Culture as well. Heraclitus expresses these same ideas elsewhere in similarly vivid terms:

> God is day night, winter summer, war peace, satiety hunger. Things change, just as when fire is mixed with incense it is called after the scent of each.

The scent produced by burning incense, in the nomenclature of complexity, is an emergent property of fire, and merely named after the substance that produces it—sandalwood, say, or frankincense, or myrrh. Interestingly, too, Heraclitus's phrasing orders these pairs of opposites schematically, moving from celestial to terrestrial to societal realms. The omission of the connective "and" (*asyndeton*, one of Heraclitus's favorite tropes) blurs any distinction between the seemingly antonymic opposites (day/night, war/peace, and so on). It is a clever rhetorical technique: to juxtapose, without a coordinating conjunction, words denoting contraries effectively conflates the phenomena those words describe, as if they were fungible points on a spectrum of experience. Heraclitus explains this point more straightforwardly thus: "Cold things become warm, what is warm becomes cold, wet becomes dry, sere becomes moist." Every qualitative state, in other words, is subject to cyclic change. He puts this point succinctly in describing the circumference of a circle: "Beginning is shared with end." For all his obscurity and paradoxes, Heraclitus is clearly trying to articulate a whole-systems philosophy. Indeed, one might even call it a "deep ecology," after philosopher Arne Naess's resonant phrase, coined in 1973, which sees "organisms as knots in a biospherical net or field of intrinsic relations."

Heraclitus's retort to his visitors that "there are gods here too" is predicated on the notion that the fire in the oven somehow partakes of the great cosmic fire that animates the universe. The idea might at first seem to fly in the face of the kind of nononsense empiricism that Aristotle recommends. But Heraclitus, for all his speculative metaphysics, was himself a staunch empiricist. "Of as many things as have to do with seeing, hearing, learning," he intones in another one of his fragments, "these I honor first and foremost." Indeed, his technique as a writer is to employ ordinary images from everyday experience to illustrate abstract concepts. What animates the ordinary and the everyday, however, is "an invisible structure," which, he says, "is stronger than a visible one." Heraclitus's word for this structure is harmony (*harmoniē*), by which competing elements are knitted together into a unity.

An observation about the sea illustrates further this aspect of Heraclitus's deep ecology:

> Sea: the purest water and most polluted; for fish, it is potable and preserving, but for humans undrinkable and deadly.

Aristotle thought statements like this one violated the Law of Noncontradiction, and so he declared Heraclitus logically incoherent, since the sea cannot possess simultaneously two contradictory attributes. But Heraclitus means simply that different organisms interact with the world differently owing to their physiological makeup. The sea, in other words, manifests different, seemingly opposite qualities in the experience of those who interact with it, in this case humans and fish, even though the sea itself is a unitary whole. For Heraclitus, the so-called unity of opposites, held together in harmony, is not a doctrine about the mystical equivalence of antitheticals. Rather, it's a heuristic statement about the fluidity and flux of phenomena in space and time and the relativity of our subjective experience. A final example will drive this point home:

> The road up, down is one and the same.

Whether the road goes uphill or downhill depends on the traveler—not only her position or orientation, but her very presence, which is required to activate its "up-ness" and "down-ness." Traveling the road, in other words, is an *event*. Indeed, the word used in Greek for "road," *hodos*, can also mean "journey," which Heraclitus might also be implying here. There is no up and down, Heraclitus suggests, only relative position, which produces a "steady state" in the moment of one's experience. This is not the same thing as relativ*ism*, the view that there is no absolute value, intrinsic attributes, or reality to things in themselves. It is, however, an idea akin to *relativity*. One blushes to invoke Einstein, Heisenberg, or Bohr on this point, but the thinking is not, as it were, unrelated.

How are metaphysics to be squared with physics, the unseen with the seen, the immaterial with the material, the speculative with what we can observe and measure? And what can any of it teach us about following Nature's lead?

Extended from a description of the world to a prescription for living, the philosophy of Heraclitus certainly provides the basis for a profounder, more durable alternative to "shallow ecology," which Naess describes with terse sarcasm: "Fight against pollution and resource depletion. Central objective: the health and affluence of people in the developed countries." Heraclitus's view, by contrast, embodies an ethos and ontology conducive to ensuring a sustainable world for everyone. There is, for one thing, no meaningful "us" and "them" in his worldview, as surely as there is no up or down. Indeed, he says himself that his philosophy's first principle, which he calls *logos*, is not esoteric knowledge, but a shared possession, "the same for all." Yes, he concedes (and frequently remarks on it), most people in this world live unthinkingly, "according to their own private understandings." But *logos* is, he says, nonetheless "common to all." None of us is exempted from its sway. That "we should pursue what is shared" is the upshot of his teaching, and the only reasonable conclusion. Remarkably for someone with such an oracular persona and misanthropic habit, Heraclitus is adamant that we should not simply take his word for it: "It is wise to listen" he declares, probably at the very beginning of his lost book, which he dedicated to the goddess Artemis at her great temple in Ephesus, "not to me, but to *logos*, and to agree that all things are one."

The word *logos* has an array of meanings in archaic Greek ranging from "word," "story," or "account" to "proportion," "measure," "mathematical ratio," and, importantly, "reason" and "rationality." "All things," Heraclitus believed, "arise in accordance with *logos*." To understand what this means and the indispensable role that reason and measure must play in living harmoniously with Nature, especially if we are to have any chance at remediating the adverse anthropogenic impacts of modernity, we turn first to early twentieth-century biology and then back again to two of Heraclitus's most influential philosophic successors, Plato, and the Stoics.

Umwelt

When zoologist Ernst Haeckel (1834–1919) coined the word ecology in 1866, he defined it as "the relation of the animal to its organic and inorganic environment." Biologist Jakob von Uexküll (1864–1944)—pronounced "oox-cool"—elaborated on this idea, dubbing these environs an organism's *Umwelt*, a bubble in which both space and time are wholly relative, experienced and navigated uniquely by each species depending on its morphology and sensory receptors. If you think that sounds a bit like Heraclitus, you would not be wrong. *Umwelt*, which simply means "environment" in German, is a crucial concept for modern ecology, and a necessary corrective to anthropic bias in human inquiry generally. Ed Yong's recent bestseller *An Immense World: How Animal Senses Reveal the*

Hidden Realms around Us (2022) documents the extent to which Uexküll's insights have taken hold of research in the biological sciences.

The poster child for Uexküll's thesis is a tiny creature that Nature lovers are bound to encounter on any walk in the woods or gambol through the grass—the ubiquitous tick. The tick has no eyes, cannot hear sounds, and has no sense of taste. It spends most of its time perched at the tip of a blade of grass or under the leaf of a shrub. Astonishingly, a tick can go for eighteen years without eating. It is stimulated to feed only by detecting the presence of butyric acid, which emanates from the skin glands of mammals. The butyric acid provides a chemical signal for the tick to drop from its perch and scurry onto whatever unsuspecting passer-by is unlucky enough have brushed up against or near where it's lurking. But that sets just the first stage of attack in motion. Contact with the hair of the animal stimulates the tick to crawl around in search of a hairless spot on the skin. Whereupon it is the sensation of warmth from the host's body—not sight or taste, for the tick lacks the requisite organs, and the butyric acid only impels it to initiate action—that triggers it to bite and feed. This explains why it's unusual to be bitten by a tick in cold weather, even if, with the warmer winters we're seeing these days due to global heating, ticks are surviving the colder months. Once the tick has gorged itself with the blood of its victim, all that's left for it to do is to detach from its host, lay its eggs on the ground and die, which it soon does.

What so impressed Uexküll, and should catch our attention as well, is that out of the hundreds of stimuli radiating from any mammal's body, only three serve as cues for the sensory recep-

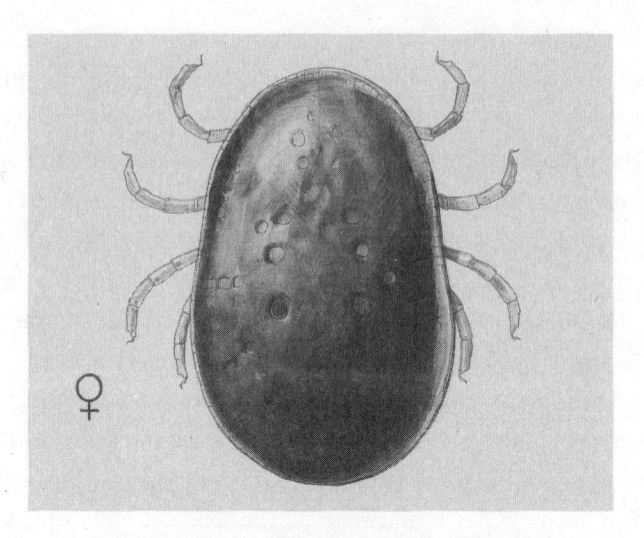

FIGURE 2.1. *Argas persicas*, scientific drawing of a
female tick.

tors available to the tick: a chemical stimulus of butyric acid
sets the process in motion; a tactile stimulus from the animal's
coat directs it to scour around until it finds a bald patch; and
heat, which induces it to bore into the skin. Remarkably, each
stimulus works in a definite sequence. What is more, the mam-
malian host is not really a passive victim at all, but an active
participant in a reciprocal scheme: it generates the stimuli in
the first place, by virtue of its own chemical and physical
characteristics.

The *Umwelten* of all organisms tell a similar tale. The tick in-
stantiates Uexküll's arresting conclusion that every creature in
Nature "lives in a world composed of subjective realities alone,
and that even the *Umwelten* themselves represent only subjec-

tive realities." This affirmation, based on scientific research on thousands of organisms, speaks volumes about agency in Nature. "Without a living subject," Uexküll writes, echoing Heraclitus, "there can be neither space nor time." Given the diversity and multiplicity of organisms on the planet, each with its own unique *Umwelt*, to say that there are many worlds and hidden realms around us is not a metaphor, or an exaggeration.

Umwelt research corroborates Aristotle's view that Nature does nothing in vain. On this point Uexküll himself is careful to distinguish between what he calls a goal and a plan. Actions and reactions in an organism's *Umwelt* are not purposeful, he suggests, meaning they are not the result of a goal the subject has in view. They are attributable rather to Nature's plan, which is the result of long co-evolutionary processes. It used to be thought, and is still commonly said, that nonhuman creatures do what they do by instinct. But instinct doesn't get us very far. It is a vacuous term, tantamount to saying that we don't know exactly how or why organisms do what they do. Ethology and even everyday observations of animals, however, give us a better inkling of what's going on than simply chalking things up to instinct and illustrate likewise the difference between a subject's goal and Nature's plan.

Here are two examples.

If you tie a chick's leg to a ground stake with a string, it will flail about trying to get away and peep vigorously. The hen takes the chick's peeping as an auditory cue that an intruder is nearby and will thrust out her beak and peck about energetically in the air around the chick, like a shadow boxer, even though there is no predator in sight. If you put that peeping chick under glass so that it is still visible but makes no sound, however, still struggling to escape its tether and in distress though it be, the hen is unfazed and goes about her business as usual, because the perceptual cue of the chick's peeping, which induces her to peck defensively, is absent. It's not her goal, in other words, to look out for her chick, come what may. She doesn't and cannot see the problem is that the chick has its leg tied to a stake. She can only act on the specific stimuli she has evolved to respond to.

Sheep behave similarly. A mother ewe knows her lambs by smell and sound, not sight. To entice a new mother into the barn after she's given birth, you need to hold the lamb to her nose and walk slowly, incrementally, to get her to follow. If the lamb is baaing, all the better. Were you to just scoop the lamb up, turn your back, and clamber off, the ewe would run about frantically, sniffing all the other lambs in the barnyard, baaing vociferously, looking for hers. The primacy of the olfactory receptor in ewes is also why the old shepherd's trick of "grafting" an orphaned or rejected lamb onto a mother who has lost one of her own by flaying her dead lamb and pulling its skin like a sweater over the orphan lamb works so remarkably well. Sheep are not stupid. They're just keen-scented.

Although the tick is a tiny insect (an arachnid, actually), the consequences and significance of the *Umwelt* thesis reverberate far and wide, even into outer space. The Webb Telescope, for example, a recent pinnacle of human technological achievement in science, throws the *Umwelt* problem into high relief, only to underscore, ironically, human limitation and frailty. Consider a graphic of the new Webb Telescope's grasp of the electromagnetic spectrum.

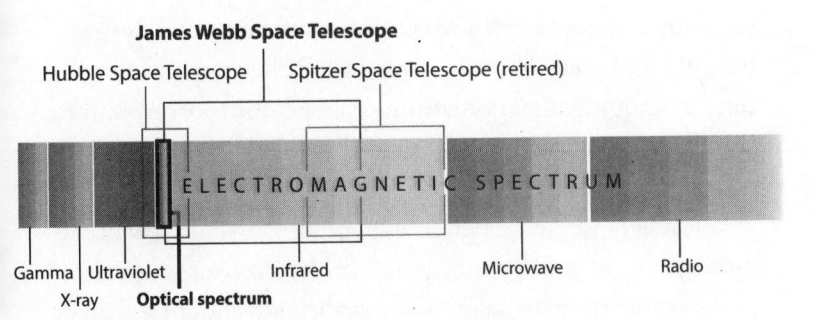

Sources: NASA; European Space Agency; Space Telescope Science Institute
WILLIAM NEFF/THE WASHINGTON POST

FIGURE 2.2. The electromagnetic spectrum.

We see that the Webb Telescope is an improvement of considerable magnitude on the Hubble, which it replaces. It can capture much more of the infrared spectrum. Yet the mere sliver of the universe's electromagnetic radiation that falls within human beings' optical window, as illustrated here, should give us pause. Most of what exists is invisible. Impressively, we have developed instruments to measure gamma, x-ray, ultraviolet, infrared, microwave, and radio frequencies. But we cannot see them. The images of planets, stars, and distant galaxies that we pore over in glossy magazines and that so inspire us are produced using false-color imaging. That is, colors within the optical spectrum are assigned to wavelengths that we cannot see to bring into view physical features that are not otherwise discernible. Slow-motion and time-lapse photography perform a similar trick to compensate for the limitations we face in processing time. The recent David Attenborough documentary *The Green Planet* (2022) utilizes new photographic techniques that can capture the growth patterns and dynamic behaviors of trees, flowers, vines, and other vegetation over time in stunning detail, revealing that plants, too, respond to stimuli in ways analogous to organisms. They, too, have their own *Umwelten*.

But it gets worse, or better, depending on your view of humanity's right and proper place in the cosmos. American philosopher Thomas Nagel, with nary a word about Uexküll or *Umwelt*, argued for a similar outlook in his classic essay from 1974, "What Is It Like to Be a Bat?" The paper, one should be quick to note, is not really about bats at all. Rather, it's a critique of reductionism in science and a demonstration of the limits of physicalism as an explanatory criterion. We cannot know subjectively, *experientially*, what it's like to be a bat, Nagel shows. The morphologies and sensory receptors of humans and bats are too alien from one another for that to be possible. Even imagining what it's like to be a bat inevitably projects human sensibilities onto the would-be experience. We get Batman, not a bat. Yet we can infer beyond much doubt that bats themselves must be capable of experiencing what it's like to be one. Nagel's verdict cuts to the chase about the significance of the issue: "Reflection on what it is like to be a bat seems to lead us, therefore, to the conclusion that there are facts that do not consist in the truth of propositions expressible in human language." And yet, he concedes, "strangely enough, we may have evidence for the truth of something we cannot fully understand." Uexküll, for one, provides such evidence with his *Umwelt* thesis. That bats possess subjective experience of what it's like to be a bat, which is beyond our own experiential reach, is proof of the existence of facts about the world that we may never apprehend.

Heraclitus, I think, would have been inclined to agree with this proposition. Although he was not an experimental scientist, he was, we have seen, an empiricist who saw glimpses in ordinary experience of extraordinary, unseen realities. Aristotle, who *was* an experimental scientist, might also have agreed, given his own penchant and ultimate preference for metaphysics. There are many differences between these two philosophers and their philosophies, to be sure, but there's also a connecting link that we need to consider, one that leads, I believe, to an ecological approach to living that unifies sensuous, subjective experience with objective, more-than-human realities. That link would be Plato.

Participation

Aristotle was Plato's student, though he rejected some of his teacher's central tenets. "Aristotle spurns me," one ancient source has Plato say about the situation, "as colts kick the mother who gave them birth." Plato (427–347 BCE) also had a mixed relationship to his predecessor Heraclitus. It is not without some irony, then, that it is he who preserves a version of one of the Riddler's most famous sayings, that you can't step into the same river twice, which Socrates quotes unfavorably in the *Cratylus* to underscore the ambiguities of significance in language. That everything in Nature is subject to change was hard for Plato to reconcile with the demonstrable truths of mathematics, a nonverbal language. Geometrically speaking, for example, a triangle, defined as a closed, two-dimensional shape with three sides, three angles, and three vertices, exists regardless of whether one has an actual object of that shape to hand. Plato was impressed by this fact and extrapolated from it: What is true and good and just, he argued, must be like a geometrical theorem, not subject to change, but subsisting in and of itself as an object of thought, always and permanently true, even if our understanding of it is only partial; whereas, the sensible world with its births and decays is an imperfect, contingent reflection or approximation of that unchanging reality. Plato developed a view about the relationship between objects of pure thought and the phenomenal world that approaches Heraclitus's ideas about the fire in the oven and about *logos*. He called it "participation," and, perhaps unexpectedly, it sheds light on what a right relationship to the environment—indeed, to the universe— might look like in the age of STEM.

Participation—in Greek *methexis*—comes from a verb that means "to be part of" or "to share in." It is an ordinary word that takes on special meaning in Plato's works when he discusses how particulars relate to universals, those abstract essences that he believed must underpin reality. These unseen universals are themselves described using an ordinary word that, paradoxically, refers to what something looks like, its visible form. Plato called them "Ideas," from the Greek verb meaning "to see." Ancient Roman readers of Plato translated Ideas into Latin as "Forms," an equivalent term.

To acquire knowledge of Ideas, we must inevitably use language and the sensory give-and-take of experience. Plato was fully aware of this fact of life, but was wary of it, because sensory experience and the language used to express it is slippery and imprecise. Wittgenstein's remark that all problems of philosophy are problems of language was not lost on Plato. The rigorous method of questioning premises, defining terms, falsifying statements— called *elenchus* ("refutation") and *dialectic* ("interrogation")—that we see Socrates deploying in Plato's dialogues is an attempt to make the best, methodologically speaking, of our linguistic shortcomings. But Plato, a voluminous author, all of whose works survive, was deeply suspicious of writing. You cannot interrupt written texts to interrogate or refute them, he points out, and writing things down lets you forget about them. Plus, as we have seen, language itself can only take you so far in the first place.

In that same dialogue in which he quotes Heraclitus on the river, the *Cratylus*, Plato summarizes the crux of the issue: "Consider, my dear Cratylus, this question, about which I often dream," Socrates says. "Shall we assert that there exists the Beautiful or the Good itself, or any other absolute reality, or not?" As in every instance where Plato floats this idea in his writings, his tone is cautious and tentative, as he is aware of the difficulties involved in proving it. "How to learn about or discover reality," Socrates admits to Cratylus, "is probably too big a question for you or me to figure out." He is more confident, however, in expressing pessimism about language's ability to capture the true nature of things, comparing those who put their trust in words to leaky pots or to people sick with runny noses—a humorous jab at the consequences if Heraclitus's dictum were true that "all things flow."

The problem Plato puts his finger on is quite simple and direct: "How can that which never stays in the same state *be* anything?" Socrates asks. If everything is always changing, it is never the same thing at any one moment and knowledge of it is therefore impossible. "We cannot even say that knowledge exists at all," he infers, "if all things are changing and nothing remains fixed." No sooner are these questions broached than the dialogue ends inconclusively with Cratylus declaring his preference for

Heraclitus's position and Socrates ambivalent about whether it might in fact be right after all. Plato shares with Nagel the view that we can at least know there are facts in this world to which we do not and perhaps cannot have direct access.

Notably, Plato does not say that Heraclitus's view is incorrect. It is merely insufficient. Sensory interaction with Nature and with other humans in a dynamic, ever-changing world plays an inevitable, but, for Plato, intermediary role in intellectual and spiritual growth, which he sees as a kind of self-actualization by reabsorption into knowledge of universal truths. This is the position taken in the *Symposium*, for example, a dialogue ostensibly about love, where sexual desire and attraction is said to be intended to arouse those keen on discovering truth to move from wanting to reproduce with beautiful bodies to consummating their desire together with the beauty of Ideas. Such is the origin of the phrase "Platonic love." Sexuality thus participates in the Beautiful (which Plato says elsewhere is also the Good)—that is, it resembles and reflects it, shares some features with it, and can motivate one toward it—but it is not reducible to it, nor its culmination or origin.

Another vivid image of Plato's notion of participation—how the physical partakes of the noetic—is his analogy in the *Republic* of the Sun as a visible image of the Good. Just as the Sun makes possible conditions for life on Earth, so the Good serves as a wellspring of moral and epistemic realities. The ecological significance of this observation is profounder than perhaps even Plato himself realized. The energy we need to live, for example, comes from the food we eat, all of which depends on plants. This includes meat and dairy, since livestock eat grass. Plants themselves get their energy directly from the Sun via photosynthesis. But why stop there?

The built environment, too, is dependent on the Sun, as steel, concrete, and glass are made from minerals, ore, and other natural resources derived from the Earth. The machines we use to build things are themselves constructed out of the same materials and run on fossil fuels, which are deposits of decomposed plants. The devices we employ to harness and seemingly to defy the laws of Nature, from smartphones to satellites, are themselves wholly natural. Even inanimate objects originate and exist because of the Sun. As one complexity scientist puts it, echoing Plato, "The Sun represents the root cause of the pockets of order that we observe around us." "The Sun," he adds, "is what helps us buck the general trend from order to disorder" in the universe.

Why order and not disorder? Because the Sun, Plato concludes, the biotic first principle, is not an independent actor but is the "offspring" of the Good, whatever that might be. Here's how he sees it:

> That which gives truth to what is known and the power to know to the knower is the Idea of the Good. It is the cause of knowledge and truth and an object of knowledge, too. Both knowledge and truth are beautiful things. But if you were to think the Good is something even more beautiful, you'd have the right idea. In the visible realm, light and sight are rightly considered Sun-like. But it is wrong to think that they are the Sun itself. So, too, in this instance: it is right to think of knowledge and truth as Good-like but wrong to think that either of them is the Good itself—for the state of the Good is yet more precious.

Ongoing discoveries in quantum mechanics only reinforce Plato's basic picture of the world, that the visible partakes of and is dependent on uncanny realities that are invisible. One conundrum among contemporary physicists is whether what we "see" when we study the universe—call it reality—is like watching a movie unfolding on the big screen or like the information stored on the film. But this Hollywood analogy is not quite as clear cut even as that, since the images are stored on the film reel as a series of isolated frames. Only when flashed quickly in succession by a projector onto the screen do they create what is called a motion picture. And the storyline itself is actualized only when we watch it.

Theoretical physicist John Wheeler (1911–2008), who gave us household terms like "black hole" and had a hand in most of the revolutionary breakthroughs in physics in the past century, described the situation in a thought experiment that you can watch for yourself in an interview on YouTube. Wheeler asks us to imagine cosmic history as the letter U painted with a calligraphic brush or in serif font, whose line begins thin on the downstroke, becomes larger at the base, thicker still on the upstroke, terminating flamboyantly in a loop at the top, through which an eye looks back at the beginning stroke.

That eye is us, gazing back at the origin of the universe. "We ourselves can and do get radiation today from the early days of the universe," Wheeler explains. "Insofar as active observation has anything to do with what we ascribe reality to, we can say this observer, who was brought into existence by the universe, has, by his act of observation, a part in bringing that universe itself into being." This is not the place nor I the person to weigh the merits or demerits of such a view, called the Participatory Anthropic Principle. But it is not fanciful speculation. The idea is based on an experimentally determined fact in quantum

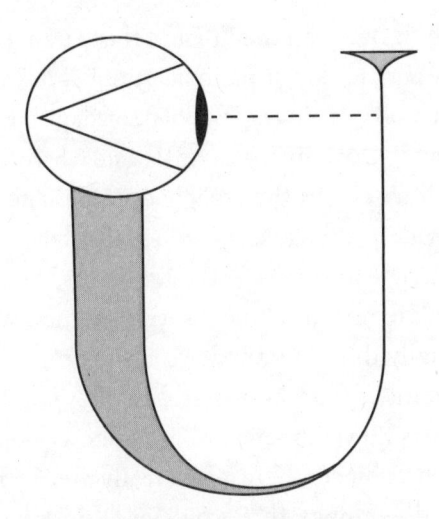

FIGURE 2.3. Wheeler's rendering of
the Participatory Anthropic Principle.

physics that particles at the quantum scale have no fixed position or even fixed characteristics until they are observed.

Plato illustrates an aspect of this conundrum with a thought experiment of his own, his justly famous Parable of the Cave, which adumbrates the quantum scenario of whether reality is situated in the film, in the projector, on screen, or created by us, the spectators. It's not an exact parallel, but the underlying issues at stake are usefully similar. Imagine a society of prisoners who live deep inside a cave, Socrates suggests, chained from childhood in such a way that they cannot turn around or move their heads from side to side, thus inhibiting even their peripheral vision. The prisoners' backs lean against a high wall or parapet—Plato compares it to the screen or curtain of a puppeteer's booth—behind which a fire burns, providing a source of light within. Between the fire and this parapet, nonimprisoned people parade along a path that runs behind and along the length of the wall carrying effigies of everyday objects high aloft on poles—images of humans, animals, and whatnot—the shadows of which are cast by the firelight onto the cave wall in front of the prisoners. "A strange scenario," says Socrates's interlocutor, Glaucus. "Strange prisoners." "They're like us," Socrates replies, then proceeds to note how under such conditions the prisoners would naturally think the shadows cast by representations of objects constitutes the whole of reality. They would think, too, that the names they happened to use to describe the shadows were what the objects themselves really are. So far removed from the truth of things, they would even mistake the echoing sounds of people chatting unseen behind the wall to be the shadows talking. Were someone to release them from their bonds, Socrates hypothesizes, and show them what was really going on, the prisoners, he suggests, would not believe it, but insist on the realness of the shadowy world that they inhabit. In a flourish that stands as the perhaps the greatest philosophical allegory of all time, Plato describes the arduous ascent from the cave to behold objects themselves in the light of the Sun. To acclimate to such a revelation, he says, would be a gradual process, as one's eyes would need to adjust to the bright light. But the revelation itself of seeing things for what they really are would impel any ex-prisoner to want to return to the cave to liberate his companions. Yet people who've known only shadows their whole lives, Plato speculates, would regard such a person as a madman whose eyesight had been ruined in the world above. They would not only disbelieve him, they'd kill him if they could. "The world we see," Plato concludes of his parable, "is like the prison dwelling. The light of the fire inside the cave is analogous to the power of the Sun. And the ascent and observation of things in the world above is like the upward journey of the soul to the realm of Ideas." And of course, it is implied, the man who sees the world as it is, returns, and is executed for his efforts to get others to follow the path out of the Cave is an after-the-fact calque for Socrates himself.

Plato's philosophic vision, like that of quantum physics, is sublime and profound, but also unnerving, alien, and abstract. What use is it?

First, let me say that whether Plato's specific propositions are true or not is, as it were, immaterial. Plato himself was unsure. As he says of the Cave, "Whether it's true or not, the god only knows." His philosophy's ecological significance is this: If you believe there is more than meets the eye in the world around you, a view Plato arrived at through reasoned argument and speculative inference, and which is in fact scientifically the case, as seen both in Uexküll's *Umwelt* and in Wheeler's U, you are more likely to treat it with intense respect, even reverence, not carelessly or with contempt. If you value the unseen as much or more than the sliver of phenomena you can see with your eyes, you're in a good position to realize that the best things in life aren't things at all. They're ideas, they're concepts, they're relationships, enjoyed in contemplation, discussion, and reflection. If that strikes you as too ethereal, impractical, or elitist, Plato, who was acutely alert to possible objections to his ideas, was not without a response to that charge, too.

The Cave allegory appears in Plato's *magnum opus*, the *Republic*, which is a work about political economy. In it, he brainstorms what an ideal human community might look like, but is immediately faced with a dilemma: Can we start with a clean slate, or must we remediate what we've already got? Plato first attempts the former, but it soon becomes apparent that the latter approach is the one the *Republic* must take. Plato's so-called First City, however, what he calls "a theoretical state built from scratch" in which "justice is found in the need its citizens have for one another," is remarkable for its down-to-Earth, rustic simplicity. "Let's look at what kind of life people who have been provided for in this fashion will lead," Socrates says to his associates.

> Won't it amount to making food, wine, clothing, and shoes? When they build their houses, they'll do their work in summer for the most part naked and barefoot, and in winter they'll be adequately bundled up with their feet shod. They'll eat barley meal that they've prepared for themselves, and wheat, baking some of it and mashing some into excellent loaves and cakes, which they'll spread out to eat on any old patch of reeds or clean leaves. Reclining on beds woven out of bryony and myrtle boughs, they and their children will feast sumptuously, then sip wine, hymning the gods. They will enjoy sex with one another, yet not produce children beyond their means, thus on their guards against poverty, or war. . . . And living life in this manner in peace and with good health they will reach old age and pass on to their progeny a life just like the one they themselves enjoyed.

If that is not the spitting image of sustainable, ecological living, I do not know what is. One of the dialogue's interlocuters objects that such a city is fit only for pigs for its lack of refined cuisine. But Socrates insists that what he describes is in fact a paradigm of the true and healthy community, whereas contemporary civilization, he says, is sick and swollen with the fever of luxury and indulgence, for which the rest of the *Republic*'s prescriptions is offered as a cure.

Plato's preference for days gone by is not a one-off. In the *Statesman*, like the *Republic* an inquiry into what constitutes political life, Plato has a character he calls "the Stranger" laud a Golden Age before the reign of Zeus where there were no states, no nuclear families, no predators and prey, and no agriculture because humans thrived by gathering plants the Earth provided of its own accord. "If people back then," Plato muses, "had had even an inkling toward philosophy or to interact with one another and with other animals in such a way as to learn from all Nature," says the Stranger, "then it would be an easy verdict to reach that people of yore were immeasurably happier than people today."

Plato is not alone. We all seem to yearn for simplicity, for a return to some prelapsarian state. One of the strongest pulls for modern students of the environment is so-called Traditional Ecological Knowledge (TEK). Beloved and best-selling books like Robin Wall Kimmerer's *Braiding Sweetgrass* (2013), David Abram's *The Spell of the Sensuous* (1997), and Elizabeth Marshall Thomas's *The Old Way* (2007) strike a chord for their celebration of Indigenous closeness to Nature. Kimmerer, an academic botanist, is also a citizen of the Potawatomi Nation who writes expressively about her experiences as a practitioner of both traditional wisdom and scientific knowledge. Abram, a philosopher and sleight-of-hand magician, extols the embodied sophistication of the Indigenous cultures he encountered while apprenticing in Southeast Asia and Indonesia. Thomas recounts with buoyant lyricism her observations living as a teenager among the Bushmen of the Kalahari in the 1950s.

Indigenous worldviews are animistic, even if they tend not to be called that these days. Whatever word we use ("cosmovision" seems now in vogue), Indigenous and other historically premodern peoples typically believe that nonhuman animals, landscapes, meteorological phenomena, even inert objects have not only agency, but personalities, and thus sentience, analogous to that possessed by humans. Such a view, one should be quick to add, while prescientific, is not, for that reason, reducible to superstition. As a species, we are all animists, or once were, since "indigenous" is synonymous with "oral." Human and proto-human communities lived, worked, and thrived for millions of years without the technology of writing. It was in symbiosis with that long period of cultural and social gestation that an animistic outlook developed. Abram, combining historical and anthropological research into the cultural consequences of writing with philosopher Maurice Merleau-Ponty's phenomenology of perception, argues that "animism was never, in truth, left behind" with the onset of literacy. "The participatory proclivity of the senses was simply transferred from the depths of the surrounding life-world to the visible letters of the alphabet." We now read marks on the page or processed information on a screen as we once read tracks in the snow or weather patterns in the sky.

It is a fascinating, compelling theory that links us cognitively to our earliest human ancestors. As is the case with literacy and orality, however, there is no going back. Indigenous cosmovisions certainly have much to reteach us about what constitutes a healthy relationship to our natural habitats. TEK itself, however, cannot offer realistic solutions to our current predicaments. An animistic worldview did not and cannot equip anyone to perform open heart surgery, transplant a kidney, or clear up a serious bacterial infection, much less get a global pandemic under control. TEK cannot feed ten billion people, to say nothing of launching satellites into space to keep our communication devices, satnav, and financial systems working. Once you've fallen off a cliff you cannot un-fall, only catch yourself, or figure out how to fly. That is the position modernity is in. We can reenchant Nature, no doubt. We can reinscribe ourselves into it and choose to cooperate with it, if not from sheer necessity, for survival, as in the old days, then at least from an ancestral sense of gratitude and enlightened self-preservation. We can make decisions today, as the Haudenosaunee put it, mindful of the aftereffects in the seventh generation. We can and we should. But we should also dispel any illusions about large-scale practical applications of TEK in the modern world.

The contemporary fascination with TEK is not misplaced. It can, however, given the nature of the social and environmental crises we face, be an exercise in elegiac nostalgia. To say that is not to discount or smooth over other issues—moral and political—of Indigenous rights of access to land, for example, of reparations for historical injury, and for environmental and socioeconomic justice in the present day. If you gathered up all the marginalized people who lay claim to Indigenous heritage worldwide today, they would comprise the planet's third most populous country after China and India. Clearly, Indigeneity is still very much with us, to our collective enrichment. But animism must become something new and different for the modern age if it is to be useful, given the technological and informational evolution that has occurred over the past 30,000 years. Whatever simplification or dematerialization of civilization we undertake to reduce our throughput and environmental impact, it must engage rigorously with scientific knowledge and political discourse. Indigenous values, to put it another way, need to be translated into modern vernaculars. Vanessa Machado de Oliveira's *Hospicing Modernity: Facing Humanity's Wrongs and the Implications for Social Activism* (2021) provides a good model.

Nonetheless, it is sobering to think that, on a time scale of over 300,000 years since the emergence of *Homo sapiens sapiens*, the invention of written language, the catalyst of modernity, is only 5,000 years old. The Scientific Revolution is 500. The digital age is barely 50. Plato can help us here. Platonic participation, I suggest, is a form of animism that can reconnect us—scientifically, philosophically, and affectively—with the world around us. Just as metaphysics springs from physics, reasoning and recursive reflection spring ultimately from an embodied co-engagement with Nature. Writing, irremediably, was a watershed. As one expert once put it, writing restructures consciousness. Indeed, to write and publish books that advocate for Indigenous worldviews is thick with irony. To write a book or blog is to engage in a supremely un-Indigenous activity, as literacy is of no interest and no use to people living in oral cultures. Yet who today would argue it is better to remain illiterate? Plato, to his credit, was acutely aware of the contradictions involved: His philosophical abstractions were made possible by literacy, yet he knew full well the then-new technology's limitations and dangers when it comes to acquiring and transmitting philosophic and political wisdom.

The theory of participation explains how what we experience, observe, and describe in the world around us is meaningful and real but only a partial aspect of a larger and largely unseen reality. The idea is not unlike the situation we find ourselves in with Newtonian physics, a useful approximation whose physical laws govern things reasonably well in the visible universe, even if quantum mechanics paints a truer picture of how things actually work. Buddhism proposes a similar solution to the problem in its Two Truths doctrine of absolute and relative truth. One later Platonist, Porphyry of Tyre (ca. 234–305 CE), in a treatise about vegetarianism and the humane treatment of animals, looks at the issue from a different angle: Do nonhuman animals participate in rational thought? Do they possess, as he says in the Greek, *logos*? His answer is that they do, and that the mistake we make with animals, as perhaps with the rest of Nature in a post-animist world, is to see the question of their rationality or sentience as an either/or, when really it is a question of degree, or, as he puts it, quoting Aristotle, "of more and less."

And so, a consideration of *logos* brings us back to animals. The role of *logos* in life is a key topic in ancient Greek philosophy. It takes on special significance for the Stoics, who took Heraclitus's early thinking on the matter further than Plato, further perhaps than any other ancient school in appealing to Nature as the yardstick against which we should measure ourselves. "Our proposition is this," writes the Roman Stoic Seneca (4 BCE–65 CE). "To live by following Nature's lead in things." Nonhuman animals, the Stoics proposed, have much to teach human animals about how to actualize that proposition.

Proprioception

Dogs, Plato had declared in the *Republic*, are true philosophers because they know instinctively what belongs in their sphere of concern and what does not. A dog differentiates instantly, he notes, between its master and its household and strangers or intruders. A philosophically minded person should be able to do the same in knowing right from wrong and how to choose the best courses of action. A habituated awareness of one's proper place in one's environment, it turns out, becomes for Plato the very definition of justice, with each part of society and one's psyche performing the tasks for which it was designed. For Plato this is the gold standard of both personal and political well-being. When he comes to name his precious Guardian class of citizens—men and women who will be specially educated to preserve a community that is organized on philosophic principles—Plato pays homage to the dog with a punning play on words: These young "Guardians" of the ideal State (Greek *phulakes*) are to be just like purebred, well-trained "puppies" (*skulakes*).

The word Plato uses in praise of dogs translated earlier as "sphere of concern" is *oikeios*, an adjective that means literally "of or pertaining to the household." As we have seen more than once already, *oikos* is a word and concept at the root of "ecology," "ecosystem," and "economics." The phrase that I render as "instinctively" is *kata phūsin* in Greek, literally "in accordance with Nature." By linking these two domains, microcosmic house and macrocosmic Nature, Plato anticipates a full-blown doctrine about the relationship between the two that the Stoics later developed called *oikeiōsis*, the process of making something "familiar" (*oikeion*) or akin to oneself. Our English word "familiar," in fact, derives from the equivalent word in Latin: *familia*, or "household."

By *oikeiōsis* the Stoics sought to describe and prescribe ways of responding to stimuli that correspond appropriately to one's nature. They argued that nonhuman animals provide instructive examples of such correspondence. Indeed, *oikeiōsis* is essentially a proto-scientific articulation of the *Umwelt* concept. Accordingly, I opt to translate this Stoic teaching with a word borrowed from neurophysiology: *proprioception*. Proprioception ("grasping what is one's own") refers to an animal's awareness of its body's position and movement in space. It is an evolutionary adaptation that allows our limbs to move into the right position at the right speed and with the right amount of force to accomplish a given task. As such it is both a conscious and a subconscious operation. Indeed, we usually take proprioception for granted, yet it contributes to our sense of balance and enables us to crack an egg into a bowl, type on a keyboard without looking, or walk and talk at the same time.

Physiologically speaking, proprioception comprises a multisensory system that involves the brain, neurons, nerves, and muscles. The Stoics ethicized the concept, seeing it as a process whereby rational agents—those possessing *logos*—give correct mental assent to what any given situation requires. Here again, etymology can be revealing: The noun *ēthos*, from which the substantive "ethics" derives, originally meant the habitual "haunt" or "den" of an animal. It is used in this sense of pigs, lions, horses, and fish, for example, in Homer and Herodotus, and of human habitats, too, in Hesiod. Only later did the word begin to be employed to describe dispositions and behavior. It is a tantalizing speculation but, given our species' long animist past, not wide of the mark to say that in the observation of animals lies the origin of ethics. Seneca, at any rate, invites us to make the connection explicit.

In a short letter of advice to his protégé Lucilius, Seneca invokes *oikeiōsis* in animals to indict human overreach and excess. "How long will we stuff the marketplaces of great cities with grain?" he complains. "How long must the masses bring in the harvests for us?" he asks, implicating those like himself who live off the labor of others. "How long must many ships convey the accoutrements for a single table," he continues, referring to luxurious lifestyles, "and these sourced not even from a single sea?" A bull, by contrast, he points out, is satisfied with the pasturage of just a few acres. One forest is plenty for many elephants. The human animal, however, must be kept fed by both land and sea. "Has Nature given us so insatiable a stomach," he inveighs further, "even though it has given us a body of such modest size, that we outstrip in greediness the most sizable animals with the largest appetites?" The clincher of Seneca's argument that human acquisitiveness and consumption are out of sync with Nature appears in a flourish at letter's end: "Let us count people like these," he surmises, "among the animals, not among humans; let us count certain people in fact not even among animates, but among the dead." The pun on the Latin word *animal* here is just outstanding. In the first instance, Seneca uses it as a noun meaning "animal"; in the second it is a substantive adjective meaning "the living" (from *animal, animalis*, which is derived from the noun *anima*, "life"), thus forming a semantic contrast, yet grammatical parallel, with "the dead."

One need not read Latin to know that *oikeiōsis* among animals is essentially an evolutionary strategy for self-preservation and survival. Human animals, however, are different from non-human ones. Nonhuman animals, the Stoics argued, act on nonrational perception. That a ewe knows to lick off her lamb after birth and to nudge it toward her udder to nurse, while the lamb knows its first task is to stand up, we call instinct, or, in more scientific terms, genetic memory. Human beings, however, act, or can act, on rational, conceptually structured perception and cognition. Humans, for example, can choose not to procreate at all. Sheep cannot. The Stoics believed that, for humans, moral excellence, or virtue, is the highest good, and that it is both necessary and sufficient in and of itself for happiness. Since humans' proprioceptive capacity is informed by reason, knowing one's proper place in the natural order of things and acting accordingly is tantamount to virtue.

The problem, however, with humans is that, because of our capacity for recursive, rational thought, we can choose to act contrary to Nature. Our emotions and irrational desires cloud and color our thinking. Instead of acting with a view toward self-preservation and true self-interest, we often opt for self-destructive attitudes and behaviors. What is more, we tend not to think for the long term or the bigger picture. To counter such pitfalls in human proprioception the Stoics proposed a classificatory system of value to determine what matters for virtuous living and what does not. They also developed elaborate psychological techniques, which they described as giving one's assent, or not, to various "impressions" that arise in the mind, to stifle the emotions' interference in rational decision making. A memorable example of such cognitive therapy is the Stoic emperor Marcus Aurelius's description of the sexual act as "merely internal attrition and the spasmodic excretion of mucus." His point is not that sexual intercourse is in fact a clinical or perfunctory experience, but that if we choose to look at it that way, from that angle, in the larger scheme of things we will not overvalue it.

With their appeal to the natures of nonhuman creatures the Stoics invite us to consider how the human animal should be interacting with its *Umwelt*—how, in other words, we might live ecologically, given the morphology and sensory receptors we ourselves possess. Since the capacity to reason is an inextricable component of our species' makeup, it must also inform our engagement with the environment we inhabit, lest we make life itself unlivable. Stoic *oikeiōsis* thus emerges as a particularly useful paradigm for reframing human belonging in the world. In that same letter to Lucilius lauding the virtues of bulls and elephants Seneca counters the uniquely human specter of the "living dead" with a Stoic definition of what it means to be alive: "That person is alive," he writes, "who proves herself useful to many; that person is alive who makes use of himself." The Stoic vision of ethical, proprioceptive living integrates the self with society. Proprioceptive values are relational values. Our cultivation of ourselves, in other words, obliges us to have regard for others as well. Marcus Aurelius puts the matter this way:

> To the extent that I remind myself I am a part of this kind of whole, I shall be quite content with all that occurs. To the degree I feel related [*oikeiōs*] to those parts that are akin to me, I will do nothing that is not in the interest of what we all share; rather, I will focus on those parts to which I am related and will direct all my energy to the advantage of our common weal.

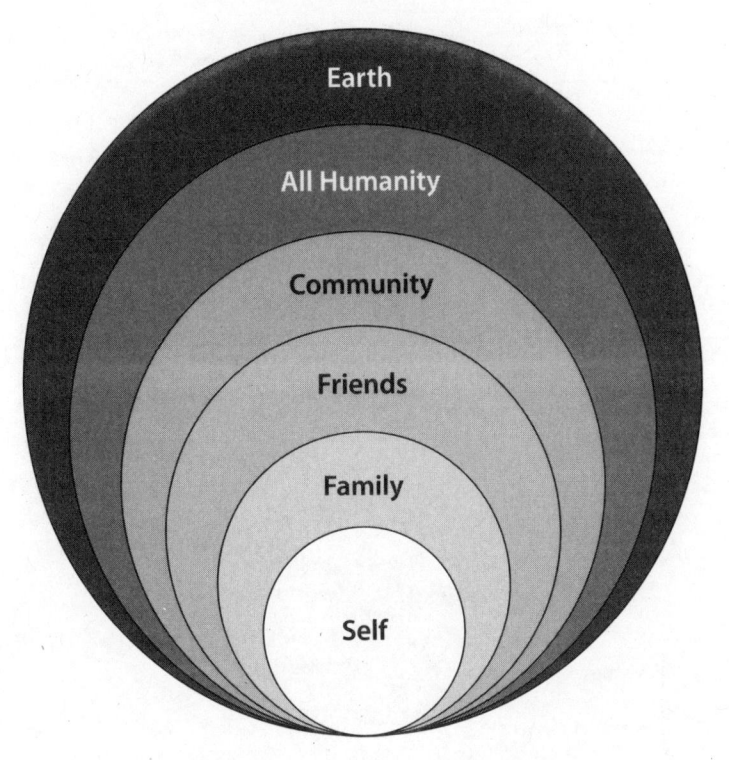

FIGURE 2.4. Hierocles's Circles of Concern.

In contrast to the vicious cycles of unlimited growth, depletion of natural resources, and externalizing costs at the expense
of the landscape and our fellow humans the Stoics exhort us to
embrace a virtuous, complementary circle involving self, others,
and the environment. In fact, to illustrate *oikeiōsis* a Stoic named
Hierocles (second century CE) employed an image of concen-
tric circles to depict our responsibilities to ourselves and others.
It is a visualization of relational priorities in the human *Umwelt*
whose goal is happiness and flourishing for all—*eudaimonia* in

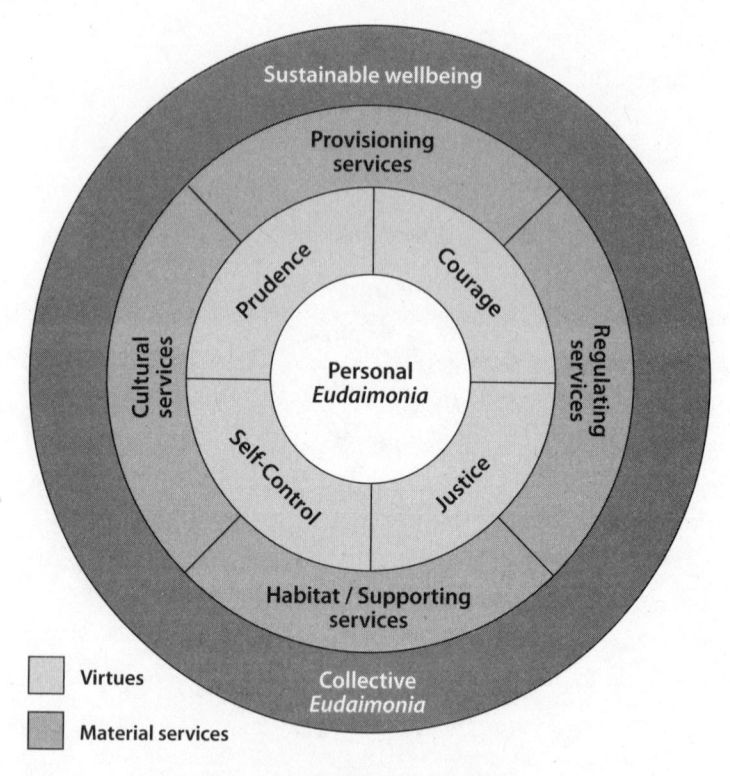

FIGURE 2.5. Hierocles's Circles with eudaimonic virtues and material services inscribed.

Greek. Kai Whiting and collaborators in Spain, writing in the journal *Sustainability*, have adapted Hierocles's diagram for the twenty-first century to bring the biosphere into the picture. Hierocles's original circles described a hierarchy of affiliations with other human persons only. Whiting's adaptation includes the natural environment—"Earth" and all that that entails.

A second mandala inspired by Hierocles depicts collective *eudaimonia* and sustainable well-being as fostered by Stoic virtues and ecosystem services. It is an image of what is possible in this world.

———

By now an alert reader will have realized that there are many aspects of Nature that we should consider unethical or unwise to imitate. Nature may do nothing in vain, as Aristotle insists, it may have a plan, as Uexküll says, but it is wholly amoral, and, from an anthropic point of view, is often violent, hierarchical, sexist, ruthless, and capricious. Nietzsche articulated this objection perhaps better than anyone, writing in *Beyond Good and Evil* (1886), "You desire to LIVE 'according to Nature'?"

> Oh, you noble Stoics, what fraud of words! Imagine to yourselves a being like Nature, boundlessly extravagant, boundlessly indifferent, without purpose or consideration, without pity or justice, at once fruitful and barren and uncertain: imagine to yourselves INDIFFERENCE as a power—how COULD you live in accordance with such indifference? To live—is not that just endeavoring to be otherwise than this Nature? Is not living valuing, preferring, being unjust, being limited, endeavoring to be different? And granted that your imperative, "living according to Nature," means actually the same as "living according to life"—how could you do DIFFERENTLY? Why should you make a principle out of what you yourselves are, and must be? In reality, however, it is quite otherwise with you: while you pretend to read with rapture the canon of your law in Nature, you want something quite the contrary, you extraordinary stage-players and self-deluders! In your pride you wish to dictate your morals and

ideals to Nature ⁞ . . . to see Nature FALSELY. . . . But this is an old and everlasting story: what happened in old times with the Stoics still happens today, as soon as ever a philosophy begins to believe in itself. It always creates the world in its own image; it cannot do otherwise.

There is no doubt that we create the world in our own image. Nietzsche himself did the same. And Nature is certainly no panacea cure for ills. But its indifference does not make it a malevolent adversary, nor our attempts to understand and relate to it false or self-serving. One finds a fairer assessment elsewhere. In *The Outermost House* (1928), written in a lonely cabin on Cape Cod while he was recovering from shell shock incurred during World War I, American naturalist Henry Beston concludes, as do I:

> And what of Nature itself—that callous and cruel engine, red in tooth and fang? . . . It is true that there are grim arrangements. Beware of judging them by whatever human values are in style. As well expect Nature to answer to your human values as to come into your house and sit in a chair. The economy of nature, its checks and balances, its measurements of competing life—all this is its great marvel and has an ethics of its own. Live in Nature, and you will soon see that for all its nonhuman rhythm, it is no cave of pain. . . . And if there are fears, know also that Nature has its unexpected and unappreciated mercies.

3

"Cosmos Out of Chaos"

"CLIMATE TRAUMA" is a phrase that has now entered the global lexicon, preceded a few years prior by "eco-anxiety," apparently a less malicious disorder. I tend to be skeptical about diagnosed psychological conditions more specific than the general malaise of the human condition we all experience to various degrees. That is perhaps my shortcoming or blind spot. But climate trauma is something else altogether. It is not a psychological or behavioral affliction arising from some innate disposition, social conditioning, or malfeasance, but a tangible, involuntary outcome caused primarily by accumulated external factors. As global temperatures rise and population densifies in settled areas, especially in the global South, the effects of catastrophic weather events like floods, hurricanes, and fires, which are increasing in frequency and intensity, are proving ever more destructive to human lives and livelihoods. This is not news. Or rather, it is news. All the news. All the time.

Take the Camp Fire of 2018. Named after Camp Creek Road, the incendiary point of origin in Butte County, California, this was no picnic with outdoors enthusiasts singing refrains of Kumbaya over hot cocoa under the stars, as its infelicitous name evokes. It was, until the disastrous Maui fires in Hawai'i last year, the deadliest wildfire in the United States since 1918 and ranks twelfth on a list of the world's deadliest. Eighty-eight human lives were lost, and countless nonhuman ones. Thousands of homes were destroyed. Over 16.5 billion dollars' worth of damage was incurred. The Camp Fire was ignited by a faulty electrical transmission line in arid conditions compounded by drought. But it was an accident just waiting to happen. The insurance companies, at any rate, can see the writing's been on the wall for some time: From 1984 to 2017 the area affected by wildfires in the Western United States has increased by 1,000 percent. That, combined with the soaring costs of new construction, has prompted companies like State Farm to place a moratorium on new homeowner policies in states like California. Making a house a home in the country's most populous state is just too risky a proposition.

A recent study, purportedly the first to examine the cognitive and neural impacts of climate trauma, concluded that individuals exposed to the Camp Fire are suffering from what its authors describe as "significant cognitive deficits" stemming from the experience quite beyond the symptoms of post-traumatic stress disorder (PTSD) that one might expect. To put it bluntly, victims' brain functions were fried along with everything else. But it does not take a peer-reviewed, clinical study to understand that traumatic experiences change us. What we do with trauma, however, whatever its source, is the decisive criterion.

Home Is Where You Hang Your Head

Consider Henry Thoreau. Not many readers will know that ten years before he became America's iconic naturalist with the publication of *Walden* (1854), Thoreau was responsible for incinerating three hundred acres in Concord Woods near Walden Pond. The fire, of course, like the Camp Fire, was an accident. Thoreau and a friend were cooking chowder in a dry stump after a morning spent fishing when their small fire got out of hand. The timber lost in the blaze was valued at $2,000, a huge sum in 1844. An entire ecosystem (though that word had not yet been invented) was destroyed. As one might imagine, Thoreau became Concord's resident pariah, earning the nickname "Woods-Burner" from the locals. Yet somehow this twenty-six-year-old Harvard graduate turned his traumatic experience at Concord Woods into a catalyst of remorse and reorientation that propelled him into his bold lifestyle experiment on Emerson's woodlot at the pond just one year later.

Thoreau's own recovery was not the outcome of clinical treatment, though he might have benefited from that, too, but the product of reading and reflection. "It is not all books that are as dull as their readers," he declares in his chapter on the subject from *Walden*.

There are probably words addressed to our condition exactly, which, if we could really hear and understand, would be more salutary than the morning or the spring to our lives, and possibly put a new aspect on the face of things for us. How many a man has dated a new era of his life from the reading of a book.

Because of their transformative potential, books, for Thoreau, "must be read as deliberately and reservedly as they were written." Life and literature should both be objects of deliberate effort and attention, as one activity informs the other. Thoreau summarizes his Walden experiment in exactly these terms, as if living were a form of literary composition or interpretation: "I went to the woods because I wished to live *deliberately*," he writes. And then he wrote a book about the experience. The books of antiquity hold special promise: "Men sometimes speak as if the study of the classics would at length make way for more modern and practical studies," Thoreau rues.

> But the adventurous student will always study classics, in whatever language they may be written and however ancient they may be. . . . They are the only oracles which are not decayed, and there are such answers to the most modern inquiry in them as Delphi and Dodona never gave. We might as well omit to study Nature because she is old.

Thoreau's linking of human intellectual history to Nature's timelines is an astute observation. Not only does it put the presentists in their place, it emphasizes the sweeping trajectory of which we form but a small part. Humanity, in fact, is a speck on the evolutionary spectrum. Over the course of our species' sociocultural development—the genus *homo* being roughly 2.5 million years young—the age of cities and civilizations is a spot upon that speck. The so-called Axial Age, 2,500 or so years ago, during which many of the world's classic works originated, is no time at all on Nature's schedule. In this sense, Homer's

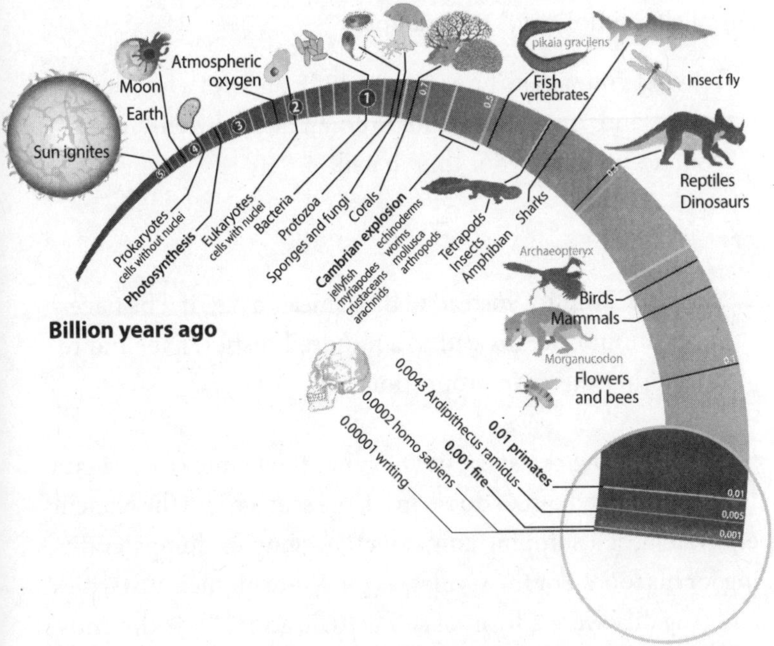

FIGURE 3.1. A textbook illustration of the Earth's
evolutionary timeline.

universe is not very far removed from our own. Indeed, it is the
same universe, seen differently.

Given the wide berth of Thoreau's perspective, it is no surprise that *Walden* teems with direct and indirect influence from
the classics, its author a walking, talking encyclopedia of Greco-
Roman commonplaces couched in a New England brogue. But
for Thoreau, the classics are not just window dressing for his
stylish prose. As for the ancients themselves, thought must be

translated into action. When Thoreau exhorts us to "Simplicity, simplicity, simplicity!" for example,

> I say, let your affairs be as two or three, and not a hundred or a thousand; instead of a million count half a dozen, and keep your accounts on your thumb nail,

or

> Simplify, simplify. Instead of three meals a day, if it be necessary eat but one; instead of a hundred dishes, five; and reduce other things in proportion,

he is channeling the spirit of Diogenes the Cynic (ca. 412–323 BCE), who lived out of doors in a large storage jar (the ancient equivalent of a shipping container), begging or dumpster diving for his food. For the Cynics, as for Thoreau, such austerities and frugality were a form of self-actualization. "It is the gods' prerogative to need nothing," Diogenes liked to say, "and so for the god-like to need only a little." Their perverse style of reasoning along these same lines produced mock syllogisms like this:

> Everything belongs to the gods.
> The wise are the gods' friends.
> Friends hold things in common.
> *Ergo*: Everything belongs to the wise.

Everything belongs to the wise—and yet the wise need only scraps and leftovers. Or consider this ancient summary of their sinuous, circuitous thinking: "Even the despising of pleasure is itself most pleasant once it's become a habit," Diogenes was keen to point out.

Just as those who've gotten accustomed to a pleasant life become miserable when they pass over to the opposite condition, so those persons whose training has been the opposite from theirs enjoy despising pleasures with more pleasure than the pleasures themselves.

That's the therapy of self-discipline. The Cynics were not the world's first ascetics, to be sure, but they have given us that word—from Greek *askēsis*, which literally means "practice" or "training." The metaphor is drawn from the idiom of ancient Greek athletics. Getting by on just a little is a form of exercise, they argued, that will strengthen you and make you impervious to the buffetings of misfortune. Any one of us, after all, could wind up homeless or find ourselves living from meal to meal. Best to prepare for it.

In contrast to other animals, the problem with *homo sapiens sapiens*, according to Diogenes and his tribe, lies in a fundamental confusion of needs and wants. We have become dependent, the Cynics argued, on unnecessary luxuries that have made us physically soft and morally weak. We are not satisfied with having our needs met but go to costly and harmful lengths in search of novelty and pleasure. To thwart such social conditioning, the Cynics cultivated autonomy by practicing self-sufficiency, or *autarkeia*. The Cynic quest for autarky is, however, somewhat paradoxically, a call to freedom through conformity—freedom *from* the injurious conventions of society by means of conformity *with* conditions found in Nature. They preferred water to wine, for example, Nature's gift as opposed to Culture's intervention, lived exposed to the elements, and even eschewed the use of fire for the cooking of food, including meat. "Nature is our whole concern," says one Cynic-tinged character in a humorous dialogue by Plutarch (ca. 45–120 CE). The speaker is called Gryllus, or "Oinker," and uniquely positioned to comment on such topics since he is one of the men whom the enchantress Circe had turned into a pig in the *Odyssey*. He has seen both sides. When asked by Odysseus if he wants to be changed back into a human being, Gryllus says No, thank you: "Why would I want to change into something worse from something better?"

To their credit, the Cynics' all-in commitment to self-sufficiency is suffused with a concern for the self-sufficiency of others. The Cynics well understood, for example, what economists now call "externalities," or the harmful side effects and human and environmental costs involved in the production and acquisition of goods. An unnamed Cynic in one ancient source likens the god in charge of this world to a host at a dinner party:

> The god is like a good host: He places before us a variety of many kinds of dishes so that we have what is appropriate for us—some things for the healthy, some for the sick, some for the strong, some for the weak—not so that we all may use everything, but so that each of us might use for ourselves what falls in our domain and, of those items, what we happen to need most.

"Whereas you," the Cynic continues, addressing his interlocuter,

> are exactly like a person who grabs everything out of greed and lack of restraint. You think it's fine to use it all, including goods from all over and not just what you have close to hand. You don't think your own land and sea are enough in them-

selves but import your pleasures from the corners of the globe and always prefer what is foreign to what is produced locally, what is costly to what is inexpensive, and what's hard to procure to what's easily acquired. . . . The many costly goods you think conducive to your happiness, over which you exult, only come to be yours through misery and suffering. That gold you pray so hard to get your hands on, the silver, the expensive houses, the finely tailored clothing, and all the accoutrements that go along with these things: How much do they cost in hardship? How much in human labor and danger, or rather, in human blood, death, and destruction? Many people are lost at sea for the sake of such things and the people who go in search for or manufacture them suffer awful fates.

The recognition of externalized costs and the preference for local goods and services over products sourced from afar enlarges on the meaning of cosmopolitanism, another word and concept the Cynics invented: The consequences of our choices, and thus our obligations to our environments and to one another, extend far and wide, and in many directions. We are inescapably "citizens of the world" and must behave as such.

A Cynic named Demetrius (10–90 CE) who was active at Rome during the reigns of Caligula and Nero ups the ante. We ravage the Earth itself, Demetrius exclaims in a street sermon preserved by Seneca, for "thin slices of two raw materials"— silver and gold—"to obtain which our greediness gropes in darkness." "And yet the Earth," he reasons,

which otherwise brings forth what is useful to us, has buried those things and sunk them deep, and lay upon them with all her weight, thinking them the most harmful substances and a bane to nations if they were to be discovered in plain sight.

"Iron is mined from the same dark recesses as silver and gold," he adds with sarcasm, "lest we lack the instrument—or the just reward—for killing one another." Allegorized to the present day, Demetrius's indictment of the extraction industry readily applies to the global crush for the silver and gold of our era—lithium, copper, nickel, manganese, and rare-earth elements with mythic names like promethium (after the Titan who gave fire to mortals), cerium (Roman goddess of agriculture), lanthanum (Greek for "hidden away"), and dysprosium ("hard to reach"), which we pillage to build our precious technologies, including solar panels and batteries for electric vehicles. To a fault, we seem prepared to do whatever it takes to avoid placing limits on economic growth or jeopardizing any pleasure or convenience. Keep the cars running! On batteries if need be! God forbid we stop selling and driving new cars. Yet depending on how your local electricity is generated, your EV could well be running on coal or fracked natural gas. Demetrius and the unnamed Cynic have turned out to be prophets of our own time, too. Yet the stakes are so much higher now given the scale of our efforts and made worse by the fact that the elements and ore required for high tech are, like fossil fuels, finite and nonrenewable. Moreover, to harvest and process these materials exacts a punishing toll on the environment and presents health risks to the human beings who mine, manufacture, and dispose of them. Given the inordinate dependence we've developed, what will happen when these resources run out—after, that is, we go through symptoms of withdrawal?

The Cynics were not scholars or writers. They were lifestylists and performance artists. Their mode of life was a philosophy of doing. They took their shtick to an extreme by acting out in purposefully antisocial ways to underscore their points. Their antics were not unlike Thoreau's refusing to pay his poll tax or not keeping pace with his companions because he heard the beat of a different drummer, only magnified by several powers. Diogenes's notorious public stunts—prowling through Athens in broad daylight holding a lamp in search of an honest person; hugging cold statues in winter and rolling around in hot sand in summer to inure himself to extremes in the weather; begging from statues to get good at being refused—were essentially enacted conceits meant to communicate something larger than the acts themselves. For doing all their private business out in the open he was called a dog by his detractors, which is what the word "Cynic" means in Greek. With typical self-effacing irony Diogenes embraced the moniker, casting himself as Athens's moral watchdog, barking truth from the sidewalks and nipping at the heels of rogues.

Thoreau announces his own Cynic credentials in the chapter "Where I Lived, and What I Lived For" with words that appear also as *Walden*'s epigraph: "I do not propose to write an ode to dejection," he sings, "but to brag as lustily as chanticleer in the morning, standing on his roost, if only to wake my neighbors up." Commentators on Thoreau see an allusion here to the medieval tale *Reynard the Fox*, or to Chaucer. A markedly similar anecdote, however, appears also in Diogenes's canon of *bon mots*. To a musician whose audience always deserted him as soon as he started to play, Diogenes is reported to have said, "Greetings, chanticleer!"—the Greek word for which is *alektōr*, "rooster." When the musician asked why he addressed him thus, Diogenes replied, "Because your song makes everyone get up!" thus scoring an ostensible insult, but one that harbors a Cynic ideal.

Still, like Thoreau, who for all his criticisms and curmudgeonly complaints about humanity croons no ode to dejection, the original Cynics were not cynical in the modern sense. They were ironists, yes, and satirists, but also realists, who saw human vanities for what they are. Because they sought actively to improve their deficiencies, one could call them optimists. They were also, despite their absurdist behavior, firm rationalists. As one ancient commentator remarks on one of Diogenes's favorite refrains: "He was constantly saying that with respect to living life one must either use one's noggin or a noose." The word I translate as "noggin" here is *logos*, a word and concept we have seen already in Heraclitus, Plato, and the Stoics, on which Diogenes puns with the word *brochos*, "noose." It only sharpens the tip of his point that *brochos* can also mean "reins." The upshot is the same: If we do not exercise reason to curb our appetites and modify our behavior, then we need physical limits or restraints; failing that, we might as well hang ourselves. In fact, Diogenes is reported as saying on another occasion, "If the human species should become extinct, there would be as much cause for regret as there would be at the annihilation of wasps or flies." From the vantage point of the biosphere (and with apologies to wasps and flies), this is undeniably true, as Nietzsche observes in his criticism of the Stoics' deference to Nature, the so-called Anthropocene be damned. A posthuman world seems one the Cynics can imagine and accept. But the story does not end there—or does not end there quite yet.

The Seneca Effect

Fire, we have seen, can be a source of psychological trauma, as it was for the Camp Fire survivors, and, perhaps, too, for Thoreau. But it is also the proverbial tester and prover of quality. A fire that destroyed the Roman colony of Lyon in 64 CE provided the philosopher Seneca with an occasion to make just this point, and to show that trial by fire is more than a byword. The attitude that Seneca suggests we adopt to cope with the precarity of collapse and the prospect of loss is especially useful in view of our current anthropogenic ailments. His analysis is so attuned, in fact, that it has inspired a scientific model that explains sudden and precipitous decline in such a way as to comprehend it and so to calibrate our inevitable participation in its making. All human and natural systems are subject to collapse. In biblical, if not apocalyptic, terms one might call it the way of all flesh.

Ugo Bardi, a chemist at the University of Florence and the model's formulator, calls it "the Seneca Effect," after Seneca's observation that "while growth proceeds slowly, the way to ruin is swift." "Would that things passed away as slowly as they take to develop," Seneca laments in his letter to Lucilius that is the source for this idea, but such is not the case: "Whatever's been built up over a long period with much effort and the gods' good graces," he explains, "a single day scatters and dissolves." Seneca offers this stark assessment to console his and Lucilius's mutual friend Aebutius Liberalis about the total loss of his city, Lyon, to fire. The destruction was so quick and so complete, Seneca reports, that "it takes longer for me to tell you it has perished than it took for the city to perish."

Lyon—Lugdunum in Latin—was an important center in Roman Gaul. The emperor Claudius was born there, as was Caracalla later. Founded in 43 BCE in the wake of the conquest of Gaul by Julius Caesar, Lugdunum was at the time of its destruction 100 years old and would have had all the magnificent temples, arenas, public buildings, baths, and grand houses of any Roman provincial capital at the height of empire. The ancient remains at Arles might give some comparative indication of its splendor. But none of that is what is important about its demise. For Seneca the annihilation of Lyon provides an opportunity to take stock of human impermanence, and, indeed, the impermanence of Nature itself. His farrago of reflections and advice on this topic reads like a letter from the past to the present day:

> We should consider nothing unexpected. Our minds ought to conduct advance reconnaissance for every situation. We should contemplate, not what usually happens, but what can happen.

> In the very midst of pleasures arise the causes of pain.

> Nothing is stable, be it political or personal. Human destinies, like those of cities, turn over in cycles.

> We should contemplate all scenarios and fortify our minds against whatever might come: Exiles, tortures, diseases, wars, shipwrecks—think on these things.

> We live in an environment that is destined to die.

Be mindful of what can happen and be cautious about it, Seneca infers. To expect the unexpected and to accept it with equanimity, however, as Seneca recommends, does not preclude us from understanding it, or even predicting it. Bardi's *Seneca Effect* (2017) charts the various growth mechanisms of complex systems, both those found in Nature and those of human design. His work, a report commissioned by the Club of Rome, uses the same "World3" modeling methods as the landmark *Limits to Growth* (1972), the Club's first published report, to show how multiple factors often compound upon one another. Feedback effects, he notes with example after example, from fisheries to fossil fuels to financial markets, can conspire to produce unanticipated collapse. While Bardi does not propose to have isolated a "Seneca equation" that captures the model mathematically, as the logistic equation has done for exponential growth, that he takes his cue from a premodern Stoic philosopher puts a reasoned response within reach of even the layperson. The specifics of systems jargon—*forcings, inputs, stocks, flows, constants, parameters, buffers, delays, attractors,* and so on—thus need not detain us. Bardi's conclusion, which is not his alone, is that collapse is not a bug. It is, as Seneca also insists, a feature of all systems. But that is not a fatalistic assertion. It's just the way things are, which we would do well to remember. There is a positive role for us to play in the unfolding drama of complexity. Indeed, as Seneca himself says about the fate of Lyon, "Often a catastrophe has simply made room for greater prosperity." We cannot reduce Nature's systems to our whims, avoid disintegration, or cheat death. But we can conform and cooperate to our just advantage.

The late Donella Meadows, whom Bardi invokes at the end of his book, the co-author of *The Limits to Growth*, enumerates a dozen places to intervene in a system to achieve desirable, sustainable outcomes. At the top of Meadows's list of what she calls "leverage points," which are contrasted with the so-called

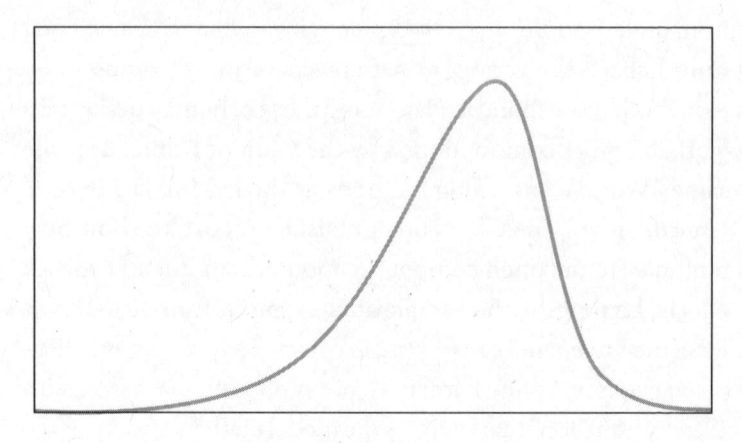

FIGURE 3.2. The Seneca Curve.

tipping points of collapse, stand the *goals* of the system, and "the mindset or paradigm out of which the system arises." As she puts it, sounding for all the world like an ethicist, not a systems modeler, "from shared social agreements about the nature of reality come system goals and information flows, feedbacks, stocks, flows and everything else about systems." "A single player," she adds, "can have the power to change the system's goal."

The Seneca Effect is a sigmoidal function, plotted as s-curves on graphs where the end point is reduced to the initial conditions at its outset.

A curve that depicts exponential growth before the Seneca Effect, well, takes effect, is shaped like a hockey stick, and the modern world is being bludgeoned to death with them. Tom Murphy, a physicist at the University of California, San Diego, musters a remarkable set of graphs depicting just this: the human population measured in billions since the year 1000; gross world product and gross world product per capita since

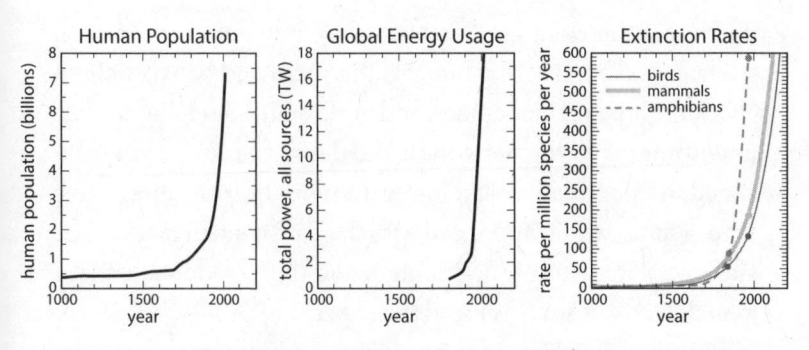

FIGURE 3.3. "Death by hockey sticks."

1800; global energy use since 1800; annual CO_2 emissions measured in gigatons since 1800; plastics discarded annually since 1950 measured in megatons; extinction rates of mammals, birds, and amphibians per year since 1400. You get the idea.

In 2021, Murphy and a multidisciplinary cohort of colleagues working in fields as diverse as anthropology, chemistry, environmental studies, and sustainable fashion design co-authored a paper published in the journal *Energy Research and Social Science* titled "Modernity Is Incompatible with Planetary Limits: Developing a PLAN for the Future." The title almost says it all. The paper, a perspective piece, besides articulating its stated premise, forms something of a manifesto for a new transdisciplinary network of scholars focused on planetary limits and the constraints such limits impose on the human endeavor. That network is called "PLAN" (Planetary Limits Academic Network), whose preliminary set of ten foundational principles include "Nonrenewable materials cannot be harvested indefinitely on a finite planet" and "Exponential growth, of physical or economic form, must eventually cease." PLAN now comprises scores of researchers from dozens of countries and US states, hailing from not just the natural sciences and engineering but also the social and behavioral sciences, the arts and humanities, and professional disciplines. A key underpinning of the network is the desire to move away from siloed, reductionist research toward more holistic, integrative scholarship. I was so impressed with the clarity and urgency of the authors' statement of the problem and their credentials that I joined PLAN as soon as I read the paper.

But one does not need to be a joiner, a scholar, or an academic to respond meaningfully to planetary limits. When Meadows speaks of "shared social agreements about the nature of reality" as the fulcrum on which to leverage a system; when she insists that a single player can affect outcomes by changing a system's goal, she says something obvious that empowers us all: Amid all the constraints we face—personal, professional, social, economic, political—we can still always choose what to think and how to respond. As Seneca himself concludes, drawing his lesson from Lyon:

> Let your mind therefore be shaped to understand and to endure its lot. Know that there is nothing that Fortune does not dare; that it has the same jurisdiction over empires as over emperors, the same power over cities as over people. There is no point in being outraged about it. This is the world we have we entered, and under such laws we live. If it's acceptable, submit to it; if not, leave; go wherever else you wish! Be outraged all you want if something unjust happens to you personally. But since this necessity is binding upon the highest- and the lowest-born alike, be reconciled to Fate, by which all things are dissolved. You should not measure human worth

by tombs, or by those monuments of unequal size that line the road. The ashes in them put us all on the same level. We are unequal at birth but equal in death. . . . To all of us, burdens to the Earth, let the same law apply: For enduring all things, we are equal; no one is feebler than another. Nor is anyone more certain than anyone else about what will happen tomorrow.

———

An equally empowering response to the prospects of collapse forms a peroration to *Walden*, which is not surprising given how much else Thoreau shares with Seneca. Seneca, for example, in addition to being a philosopher-poet, was, like Thoreau, an avid naturalist, writing seven books of "research into Nature" (*Naturales Quaestiones*). Indeed, in his keen observation and love of the natural world, Thoreau is even closer to Seneca than to the Cynics, sharing with him, too, the philosophy of self-reliance and of following Nature's lead. Unlike Seneca, however, Thoreau, living as he did on the cusp of an industrialized, mechanized age, finds Nature's beauty and restorative power at work in even the built environment. Given the scale of today's human imprint on the planet, that is a realization that needs to dawn on us, too.

The Deep Cut

A year before Thoreau burned down Concord Woods, the Fitchburg Railroad laid down tracks near Walden Pond for its line connecting Boston to Fitchburg. The original Fitchburg

FIGURE 3.4. Herbert Wendell Gleason, *The Fitchburg Railroad and Walden Pond in Winter, Concord, Mass.*, March 24, 1920.

Line, at 54 miles long, was, until 2010, the longest run in the present-day MBTA Commuter Rail system. And it is one of the oldest railways in New England. By 1900, fortunes swelled and the Fitchburg's Hoosac Tunnel Line took passengers and goods westward toward Chicago. The Lake Champlain Route connected Boston to points north like Burlington, Vermont, the metropolis in my own backyard.

The Railroad was literally a fixture in Thoreau's landscape. Its tracks pass remarkably close to Walden Pond, and the Fitchburg Line—both its reality and the specter of it—is practically a character in his writing: "I usually go to the village along its causeway, and am, as it were, related to society by this link,"

FIGURE 3.5. Herbert Wendell Gleason, *Sand Foliage
from Deep Cut on R.R. (Railroad), Concord, Mass.,*
March 17, 1900.

Thoreau writes in "Sounds." The engine's whistle, he complains, pierces the still silence of his idyllic retreat like a screaming hawk circling a farmer's field. The billowing smoke of "this cloud-compeller," he adds, cribbing an epithet from Homer, announces its arrival from afar as it were an epiphany of the angry storm god Zeus.

Thoreau's frequent walks into Concord along the railroad tracks took him through a heavily excavated stretch of the line known as the Deep Cut, to which he returned again and again each year in early spring, even after leaving his cabin at the Pond, to observe and to take notes. He was fascinated by the leaf-shaped sand flows and trickling surface erosion caused by melting frost in the embankment. Herbert Gleason's near-period photographs give some idea of what captured Thoreau's imagination.

The chapter in *Walden* titled "Spring," what one scholar has called "the high point of Thoreau's epic," is a rapturous paean to these formations that celebrates Nature's irrepressible vigor. Lurking within his lengthy description of this sand foliage is nothing short of a philosophy of life that is as ancient as it is urgent for humanity to adopt today. It's the worldview of restoration ecology and of optimistic resignation in the face of dynamic change caused by anthropic interference. It is inspired and guided by Nature's capacity for resilience.

"The coming in of spring," Thoreau announces, "is like the creation of Cosmos out of Chaos." This one sentence contains the kernel of the whole idea. The word *cosmos* means "order" in Greek. The notion of it emerging from *chaos*, another Greek word meaning "gap," or "void," is an idea borrowed from the Greek poet Hesiod (seventh century BCE) via the Roman poet Ovid (43 BCE–17 CE). Thoreau's evocation of Ovid, a passage from whose *Metamorphoses* he translates to illustrate what he means by Cosmos from Chaos, combined with his use of both words in marked uppercase, underscores that his vision of creation is not only poetic and mythological, but harks back to the speculative, proto-scientific research of Presocratic philosophers like Heraclitus, as indeed does Ovid's own. In modern scientific terms, at any rate, the emergence of order out of seeming chaos is the very definition of complexity, of which the sand foliage is an emergent property. As Thoreau puts it, "It is wonderful how rapidly yet perfectly the sand organizes itself as it flows"—self-organization being one of the hallmarks of complexity.

Contrary to what one might expect, it is not a glorious sunrise or a proliferation of daffodils stretching o'er vales and hills that inspires Thoreau's reverie, but this self-organizing feature in a sandbank created by the Deep Cut, an outgrowth not of Nature but of human intervention.

"When the frost comes out in the spring," Thoreau observes,

and even in a thawing day in the winter, the sand begins to flow down the slopes like lava, sometimes bursting out through the snow and overflowing it where no sand was to be seen before. Innumerable little streams overlap and interlace one with another, exhibiting a sort of hybrid product, which obeys half way the law of currents, and half way that of vegetation. As it flows it takes the forms of sappy leaves or vines, making heaps of pulpy sprays a foot or more in depth, and resembling, as you look down on them, the laciniated, lobed, and imbricated thalluses of some lichens; or you are reminded of coral, of leopard's paws or birds' feet, of brains or lungs or bowels, and excrements of all kinds. It is a truly *grotesque* vegetation, whose forms and color we see imitated in bronze, a sort of architectural foliage more ancient and typical than acanthus, chiccory, ivy, vine, or any vegetable leaves; destined perhaps, under some circumstances, to become a puzzle to future geologists.

As with nearly every paragraph in Thoreau, this one repays close attention. Books, after all, need to be read as deliberately and reservedly as they were written. "Excrements of all kinds," for example, is a supremely learned pun that is worth dwelling on. The Latin word *excrementum* has two derivations. It comes primarily from the verb *excerno*, and thus literally "what is sifted out." Hence the meaning "refuse," "waste," or "feces." But another, distinct word *excrementum* derives from *excresco* ("to grow forth, rise up"). The entry in Forcellini's Lexicon (1831), to which Thoreau had access, makes this all very clear, as does Ainsworth's Latin dictionary, which he owned. By the time Thoreau's sentence here has unfolded, moving as it does from sappy leaves and vines to pulpy sprays, imbricated thalluses, lichen, coral, leopard's paws and birds' feet, to brains, lungs, and bowels, we realize that when Thoreau says "excrements of all kinds" he means the word in both senses, namely *outgrowths*, a sense that fits the semantic domain of the animals and plants in the first half of the sentence, and *waste products*, which "brains," "lungs," and especially "bowels" call to mind (as does Gleason's photograph).

To call the sand foliage a "truly *grotesque* vegetation" underscores the pun on "excrements" while creating another *double entendre* hard on its heels involving the word *grotesque*. That word, too, has two senses. In Thoreau's time, as today, it primarily meant "ugly" and connoted "disgusting" (in the way that excrement is disgusting). But its original meaning, from Italian *grottesco*, is "of or pertaining to a cave." The word was coined by artists and writers of the Italian Renaissance in conjunction with the accidental discovery—by then buried underground—of the emperor Nero's notorious Domus Aurea, or "Golden House." Painters like Raphael and Michelangelo, eager for inspiration from the past and armed with torches, were lowered down by ropes into cavities in the ground (across the street from where the Colosseum stands today) that contained colorful wall paintings with ornate vegetal borders and decorations. These recesses, in fact, were actually rooms in the Domus Aurea, which had been buried long before (and intentionally so), first by the emperor Trajan, and then also by centuries of further destruction and reconstruction above ground. That Thoreau has in mind the art-historical sense of *grotesque* is clear from his appeal to the "forms and color we see imitated in bronze, a sort of architectural foliage more ancient and typical than acanthus, chiccory, ivy, vine, or any vegetable leaves."

Today one can see the earliest and most influential adaptations of Nero's grotesques in Raphael's painted loggias in the Vatican. However, this kind of decoration also appears on Corinthian columns and on other architectural elements the world over. Eventually the style made its way across centuries from the palaces and temples of the great onto everyday household furniture. In "Sounds," for example, Thoreau describes his first spring cleaning. He empties his cabin, putting all its furniture outside amid the trees while he sweeps and muses puckishly:

> A bird sits on the next bough, life-everlasting [a kind of flower] grows under the table, and blackberry vines run round its legs; pine cones, chestnut burs, and strawberry leaves are strewn about. It looked as if this was the way these forms came to be transferred to our furniture, to tables, chairs, and bedsteads,— because they once stood in their midst.

The image Thoreau conjures here is of decorative forms drawn from Nature emerging spontaneously on his furniture owing to its proximity to their source. "I did not remove the books and pen and ink," he adds, inscribing himself into the scene, "standing amid the pines and hickories. They seemed glad to get out themselves, and as if unwilling to be brought in. I was sometimes tempted to stretch an awning over them and take my seat there."

What is noteworthy in both passages—an idea embedded in the puns themselves—is the equivalence or interdependence of growth and decay that these comparisons suggest, which Thoreau validates as integral, reciprocal aspects of the same organic process. "We can never have enough of nature," he declares. "We must be refreshed by the sight of inexhaustible vigor, vast and titanic features." For all his puns and rhetorical flair, Thoreau seems awake nonetheless to the pitfalls and dishonesty of any simplistic, uncritical embrace of Nature in its awesome totality. Yes, this is the man who famously pronounced in his essay "Walking," originally composed and delivered as a lecture to the Concord Lyceum in 1851 but published posthumously only in 1862, "In Wildness is the preservation of the World." Here Thoreau attenuates somewhat: "We need a tonic of wildness" he says—a *tonic*, a medicinal—but along with it an underlying, sober respect for what he calls "the strong appetite and inviolable health of Nature." The stench of a dead horse by the road, the sight of a vulture gorging itself on carrion, creatures "squashed out of existence like pulp," tiny tadpoles quaffed down whole, toads and turtles splotched on the road are all quotidian signs of Nature's prodigality—"so rife with life," Thoreau reflects, "that myriads can be afforded to be sacrificed." The thought of prodigal and prodigious Nature is perhaps, as he says, a "compensation" for the experiential reality of such things, but it cannot prevent them from happening. As Thoreau puts the matter in "Economy," prefiguring Whitman, "The better part of the man," too, "is soon ploughed into the soil for compost."

And yet, for all this, Nature is absolved by what Thoreau calls its "universal innocence," a compressed phrase that stretches the senses of both "universal" and "innocence." "Universal innocence" does means that everyone is innocent, but that the universe does not cause harm by malice or intent. Thoreau puts the same idea differently a few sentences earlier in this passage when describing Nature's destructive prowess where he uses the language of insurance, accounting, or reckoning: "With liability to accident we must see how little account is to be made of it." In saying further that, in view of Nature's titanic vigor, "poison is not poisonous after all, nor are any wounds fatal," Thoreau approaches a view of Nature we find also in Heraclitus as a paradoxical unity of opposites held in dynamic tension. Similarly, three final sentences in this section, cryptic on the surface, also Heraclitean in tone, become more transparent when one sees Thoreau's etymological plays on the leading words and the worldview he is trying to convey: "Compassion," he concludes, "is a very untenable ground"—*untenable*, from Latin *teneo*, means here ground that "cannot be held or occupied" because it is not stable or conducive to settlement, not that human compassion is untenable in that it is unreasonable, or illegitimate. "It must be expeditious," he adds—*expeditious* as in compassion needs to "get out from underfoot" (*ex-pedio*) on such shifting sands. We should be wary, in other words, of anthropomorphizing and thus misconstruing Nature's designs. "Its pleadings will not bear to be stereotyped" he concludes. *Stereotyped*, from Greek *stereos*, "solid, firm" + *tupoō*, "to stamp, impress," means literally that pleadings based on compassion cannot be "impressed on a solid surface," because, as noted moments earlier, that ground is "untenable." The general sentiment, and the principle that appropriate ethical and emotional responses should derive from physical realities, accords closely with the Epicurean view and with Heraclitus's doctrine that "everything flows." It is, above all, an example of following Nature's lead that should strike awe in us, one perhaps of which even Nietzsche might approve.

At the outset of his description Thoreau infers that sand foliage as he observed it in the Deep Cut is "a phenomenon not very common on so large a scale" ("a quarter of a mile on one or both sides"). As we have seen, size in complex systems matters (Anderson's "more is different"; Engels's law of the transformation of quantity into quality), as does scale, as does the relationship of macrocosm to microcosm and of parts to whole. Thoreau's statement here implies all this. The man-made sandbank created the conditions for Nature to run its course as it does without human interference on smaller scales elsewhere under similar conditions. Thoreau makes some profound and perceptive remarks about scale elsewhere in this chapter, too, that are sprung from his close and systematic observation of Walden's environs: "The phenomena of the year take place every day in a pond on a small scale." "The day is an epitome of the year." "The largest pond is as sensitive to atmospheric changes as the globule of mercury in its tube."

Despite the unusualness of the Deep Cut, Thoreau concedes that "the number of freshly exposed banks of the right material must have been greatly multiplied since railroads were invented." Since railroads were invented! What Thoreau might have said today, where human imprint and infrastructure has compounded itself by exponential growth beyond the Earth's carrying capacity, where the mass of human-made objects outweighs the biomass of the planet, one can only imagine. And yet the lesson from the Deep Cut is as fresh today as it was visionary then: The Railroad, a product of Culture, produces a marvel of Nature; Thoreau encounters this natural wonder while walking from the wilds of Walden Pond to the village, his track, paradoxically, the steel trappings and wooden ties of industry. No matter where we live, that's our world today: The built environment encroaches on natural areas at every turn. One domain impinges on the other. We should leverage that unavoidable fact to the advantage of both settings without detriment to Nature, the source of our settled, civilized life and so our priority. Or so it should be.

The vista of the Deep Cut is also reminiscent, however, of Edward Burtynsky's panoramic photographs of junk heaps, factory sprawl, extraction pits, and toxic wastelands: Beautiful, natural-looking forms and patterns emerge from industrial detritus and decay and the photographs convey an eerie, Ansel Adams–like sublimity, despite the human exploitation of Nature that they depict.

Resilience in Nature can, if we follow its lead, serve as a model for our own responses to climate trauma and all the other residuals caused by modern lifestyles. Krakatoa, the small Indonesian island that was destroyed by a massive volcanic eruption in 1883, is a case in point. That eruption spewed volcanic dust over the whole planet, affecting weather patterns as far away as Los Angeles, California. The blast itself and the tsunamis that followed in its seismic wake wiped out over 36,000 people. One year after the eruption scientists could find only one spider and a few blades of grass on the remains of Krakatoa. Twenty-five years later, however, 202 species of animal were catalogued in a three-day expedition. Fifty years on, 880 animal species were flourishing, and a small forest covered the island. The volcanic eruption and new efflorescence of life afterward at Mount St. Helens in Washington State tells a similar story.

The dormant slag heaps, or terrils, of the Nord-Pas de Calais region of France, which in 2012 joined the Pyramids of Egypt as a UNESCO World Heritage site, are an even closer parallel. Hundreds of terrils, some of them as tall as 150 meters, are scattered among now deserted model cities, which were purpose-built as utopian worker communities in the nineteenth and early twentieth centuries to support the region's 300-year-old coal mining industry. UNESCO describes the Nord-Pas de Calais Mining Basin as a precious, "organically evolved" cultural landscape "uniquely representing the combined work of nature and of man." A new and vibrant ecosystem has sprung up on the terrils since active mining ceased in the 1960s. In the village of Rieulay, for example, a goat farmer has put down roots and built *Chevrerie des Terrils* ("Slag-heaps Goat Farm"). He grazes his animals on the spoil tips, which produce brushy fodder that is ideal for goats. A vintner has established a vineyard among the so-called overburden and coal tailings. It is France's northern-most estate and produces a fine "Charbonnay." The growing conditions are reportedly superb for vines: The gravelly black soil promotes good drainage and retains heat. Ecosystems can be fragile, and 300 years of coal mining will take its toll, but Nature is resilient. As one resident puts it, "At the end of the day, what is a terril but a hill of stones that we took from nature, from underground? Well now we are giving it back to nature.

And nature then gives it back to us once again, by bringing flowers, and trees, and animals."

All this could be cause for hope. Thoreau compares standing there and looking at the Deep Cut to being "in the laboratory of the Artist who made the world . . . strewing his fresh designs about." It's a vivid metaphor of re-genesis that finds actual, contemporary expression in the work of bioengineer and designer Neri Oxman, who in the experimental structures and objects she creates is trying to replicate the kind of synergistic cooperation with natural processes that the Deep Cut produced of its own accord. Is her facility at MIT a studio or a lab? The question arises only because Oxman's work is at once high art and high tech. Her Silk Pavilion II project is a good example, and answers a key design question she poses to herself and to us: "What if human-made and Nature-grown were indistinguishable?"

Silk Pavilion II was commissioned by the Museum of Modern Art in New York City for its exhibition *Material Ecology* in 2020. Oxman and her team introduced Italian-bred silkworms onto a soluble mesh substrate stretched over a lightweight, cylindrically shaped armature of wire. They built a steel mandrel with wheels at either end to rotate slowly, clockwise, mimicking the caterpillars' kinetics in the cocoon, while the silkworms—15,532 of them—worked away on the mesh. (The sleek contraption resembles a spaceship from take-your-pick science fiction.) In Nature, silk caterpillars spin themselves into a cocoon before metamorphosing into a moth. To harvest individual silk filaments from cocoons one must boil them, to dissolve the sticky adhesive that binds the layers together, thus killing the silkworms inside. Those single threads are what are then spun into fabric. On the rotating jig, however, spinning and weaving becomes a single process, and no silkworms are exterminated. Oxman's achievement is the discovery that human-manufactured structures can influence silkworms to spin in sheets instead of cocoons, producing thereby the same quantity of finished silk without boiling and aborting the life cycle of the larvae. "The project," she reflects, "illustrates how these compact and unique insects can act not only as living looms but as co-designers collaborating with humans to design and construct architectural-scale structures embodying co-fabrication for cohabitation."

Oxman's creations, like Silk Pavilion II, are ingenious, and beautiful to behold. Her guiding principles of cooperative design are both visionary and exemplary. It is at the risk of appearing contrarian, then, that I throw out the caveat that the energy, infrastructure, machines, and materials we use for research and development and to manufacture innovation are not usually themselves innovative or eco-friendly. Indeed, the environmental footprint of the whole scientific enterprise is considerable. Arguably, this inevitable trade-off is an acceptable up-front investment for developing resource-conserving and ethically sound returns. Another approach to innovation, however, easily sourced and often cost-free, is what is now touted as "low-tech," but which entered modern discourse with the name "appropriate technology." The concept was promulgated by E. F. Schumacher, author of the classic *Small Is Beautiful: Economics as if People Mattered* (1973). The idea came to him in the 1950s and 1960s while he was working as chief economist for the British National Coal Board and as a consultant to former British colonies in South Asia. Schumacher was inspired by the All-India Spinners Association, the brainchild of Gandhi, which was founded to support India's economic independence from Great

Britain by promoting self-sufficient, small-scale, local production and consumption of goods, symbolized by traditional homespun cloth. Gandhi himself spent part of each day in later life at the spinning wheel and the humble mechanism almost made it onto the Indian national flag. (It was later replaced by the Ashoka Chakra, or dharma wheel.)

Schumacher himself used the term "intermediate technology," by which he meant a technology superior to inefficient, rudimentary tools and practices, yet one "simpler, cheaper and freer than the supertechnology of the rich." The thrust of the idea is never to use more than you need, of either labor or materials, to get a job done. Doing so eliminates both waste and unnecessary energy input and expense. Philosopher Ivan Illich used the word "convivial" to describe the proper human relationship to technology. His *Tools for Conviviality* (also 1973) advocates for the expansion of technology the average person can employ to accomplish the everyday tasks of living without elaborate gadgets designed and commodified by elite specialists. Today a veritable bible in four volumes (2,398 pages, 709 images) of low-tech solutions for modern living is available from Kris De Decker, a Belgian eco-journalist living in Barcelona. De Decker publishes *Low-Tech Magazine*, whose website runs on a solar-powered server that is, appropriately, weather-dependent. De Decker himself lives in a small apartment atop a bar and produces his own electricity with a bicycle generator. In many respects, De Decker's magazine is a pan-regional, transhistorical version of the popular *Foxfire* anthologies (1967–), which document in a how-to format the traditional, resourceful arts and crafts of Appalachia, where you can learn how to dress a hog, build a log cabin, or make a banjo.

Low-tech is not a gimmick. Like Gandhi's All-Spinners it's as much or more about autonomy as it is about conservation, the pursuit of the one, paradoxically, conducive to the other. Limits, it turns out, can be liberating. This is quite different from one prevalent view of freedom as the pursuit of happiness, defined as doing whatever you want so long as it doesn't prevent others from doing whatever they want, which has in practice produced the opposite of freedom in the economies of late capitalism. Who would have thought that following Nature's lead might be political?

Thoreau was on to low-tech and resource conservation long before it was a thing, or even needed to be a thing. As he relates in detail in his chapter "Economy," he built his cabin with boards that he harvested for reuse by carefully disassembling a neighbor's shanty. Anticipating Oxman, he speaks of the function of human clothing in botanical, biological terms as "cuticle," "epidermis," "cellular integument," "cortex," and "bark." He lacked only the know-how, or the nerve, to design them as such—though Oxman has. His verdict on shelter is also illuminating. After several admiring paragraphs about the comfort and sophistication of Native American wigwams, Thoreau avers:

> If it is asserted that civilization is a real advance in the condition of man,—and I think that it is, though only the wise improve their advantages,—it must be shown that it has produced better dwellings without making them more costly; and the cost of a thing is the amount of what I will call life which is required to be exchanged for it, immediately or in the long run.

Even a large box he once noticed some railroad workers using to store their tools, "six feet long by three wide," essentially the size of a coffin, struck him as a serviceable abode:

> Every man who was hard pushed might get such a one for a dollar, and, having bored auger holes in it, to admit the air at least, get into it when it rained and at night, and hook down the lid, and so have freedom in his love, and in his soul be free.

This is yet another Cynic trope: The kind of large terracotta storage jar that Diogenes had repurposed as his house, a *pithos*, was also used to bury the dead, making Diogenes's choice of accommodation not only a gesture of frugality and resourcefulness but also a statement of the philosophic commonplace that one's life is a preparation for death.

Thoreau, despite his youth and other shortcomings, was a rare bird, at one and the same time a complexity thinker and simplicity advocate of low-tech. That's a combined approach to living we need to rediscover. Innovate to shrink, not to grow. Think big and systemically on small, local scales. Cosmos can arise from Chaos even without the advent of spring. In constructing this lifestyle, this philosophy of life, Thoreau was emulating the ancients. Indeed, one of the most impressive aspects of philosophy in antiquity—and this is true of every school, no matter how refined or metaphysical its doctrines—is the insistence that human beings should consume less, thus conserving more, which is remarkable given the comparatively insignificant impact ancient societies had on the environment compared to our own. One can make all the assertions one wants about environmental damage in antiquity—the deforestation of Thrace to build warships, species extinction throughout the Mediterranean region and Africa from overhunting and gladiatorial gaming, soil erosion, overfishing, pollution from the mining and processing of ore. It is now a cottage industry in archaeology and ancient history to try to find examples of today's environmental rapacity and climate crisis in antiquity. Titles like *Environmental Problems of the Greeks and Romans* are just the tip of that melting iceberg. But it takes a PhD in common sense alone to see that the ancients' global impact was nothing compared to what ours is today. That our most thoughtful forebears decried consumption, extravagance, and excess and eschewed it with such vigor—on ethical grounds, as well as practical ones—is a scolding to us.

On this score Thoreau cites an anecdote about Bias of Priene (sixth century BCE), one of the Seven Sages of ancient Greece, who were what you might call proto-philosophers. (Thales of Miletus and Solon of Athens were counted among their ranks.) He had read about Bias, whom he calls "the old philosopher," in his friend Bronson Alcott's copy of François Fénelon's popular compilation *The Lives and Most Remarkable Maxims of the Ancient Philosophers* (1702). "Our dress," Thoreau writes in his journal, a note that made its way into *Walden* in his discussion of appropriate attire,

> should be such as will hang conveniently about us, and fit equally well in good and in bad fortune; such as will approve itself of the right fashion and fabric, whether for the cotillion or the earthquake. In the sack of Priene, when the inhabitants with much hurry and bustle were carrying their effects to a place of safety, some one asked Bias, who remained tran-

quil amid the confusion, why he was not thinking how he should save something, as the others were. "I do so," said Bias, "for I carry all my effects with me."

Armed with nothing, one can, or could, at any rate, walk away from a disaster like the Camp Fire, the sack of Priene, or the burning of Lyon unscathed, for, not only is Nature resilient, but, as Seneca says, sometimes a catastrophe simply makes room for better things; or, as Diogenes put it, it's the gods' prerogative to need nothing but for the god-like to need only a little.

4

"There Is No Wealth
but Life"

WHAT IS THE PURPOSE of a human economy? How can an economy cooperate with Nature to further the well-being of all humanity and the environment?

If these questions sound naïve for the twenty-first century, or out of bounds for a classicist, tough luck, because they should be front and center for anyone who loves life, given that human economic expansion and growth over the past 150 years is the direct cause of the dangerous blight that is upon us. What began as normal species interaction with the natural world, facilitated by the gainful use of appropriately scaled technology, to obtain resources that support human lives and livelihoods, has spiraled out of control, and now threatens to make our planet unlivable. I am wary of exaggerating the point, but to our detriment we have come to worship the growth economy as if it were a god—an impersonal god, to be sure, but omnipotent nonetheless, an Unmoved Mover plying an invisible hand by whose power all things are set and stay in motion. We either bask in its beneficent light, or flounder on its choppy seas. Everyone is at its mercy.

As with all gods, however, we have made this one, too, in our own image, a projection of human hopes and fears, meaning we can also unmake it, or remake it according to a new pattern, a new image, one that sees Nature and fellow human beings as ends in themselves, not means to something else. Two most unlikely suspects, each grounded in ancient, premodern ways of thinking, offer compelling analysis and some surprisingly fresh ideas about what a human economy is for, and how it, like us, can follow Nature's lead. Neither was a credentialed economist, yet both are nonetheless original and important ecologically minded philosophers of economic concerns. John Ruskin (1819–1900), hardly a household name now, was a prolific Victorian polymath and social reformer, best known as an art historian and critic. Georges Bataille (1897–1962) could not be a more dissimilar character. Equally polymathic, Bataille is perhaps unfairly remembered, if at all, primarily for his youthful experiments in scatological fiction. He remains, notwithstanding, a serious thinker.

Ruskin's ideas sprang from his lifelong love of Nature and his admiration for the medieval democratic merchant state of Venice and the craftsmanship and ingenuity that built its prosperity and its monuments, including St. Mark's Basilica. Bataille derived his economic insights from an anthropological fascination with the earthier aspects of human experience, often expressed as ritualized, sometimes transgressive, behavior, or in the symbology of art, which might (or might not) seem surprising for someone who earned his living as a librarian. Ruskin's broadside

Unto This Last (1862) and Bataille's "Theory of General Economy"—his book *La Part maudite* ("The Accursed Share"), published in 1949—are early, unacknowledged landmarks in the field of ecological economics, a contemporary offshoot of the parent discipline that coalesced around the works of Adam Smith (1723–1790), David Ricardo (1772–1823), and John Stuart Mill (1806–1873). Punching above their weight, Ruskin and Bataille, each in his own way, counter so-called classical economics with ecology and the classics.

The Trophic Pyramid

The foundation for understanding Ruskin's and Bataille's thought is the simple fact that, in biophysical terms, an economy is, fundamentally, nothing more or less than a system in which energy is circulated and distributed. This observation should be uncontroversial, yet it is surprising how energy-blind our societies have become, despite being wholly energy dependent. Some of this blindness is willful, some of it stems from ignorance. In my hometown, for example, I recently saw the delivery truck of a local fuels supply company with "Energy Alternatives" emblazoned as its new slogan on the side—in old-timey lettering, since this family-owned business has been serving our area since 1930, when the fuels of choice were firewood and coal. But the fact of the matter is that there are no alternatives to energy, in either the natural or built environments. There are options about what kinds of energy to use, but not alternatives.

The point is well illustrated by a fundamental concept in ecology first proposed by Karl Gottfried Semper (1832–1893), developed by Charles Elton in his classic *Animal Ecology* (1927), and later substantiated, quantified, and formalized further by Raymond Lindeman in a now famous paper from 1942 titled "The Trophic Dynamic Aspect of Ecology." The paper, a chapter from Lindeman's University of Minnesota PhD dissertation from the year before, was initially rejected by the journal *Ecology* and only published posthumously after a senior colleague at Yale intervened with the editor. (Lindeman himself died prematurely at age 27.) Lindeman's research at a senescent lake, Cedar Bog Lake, now part of the Cedar Creek Ecosystem Science Reserve in East Bethel, Minnesota, was groundbreaking, and became the basis for a model of nutrient cycling that Lindeman quantified with empirical data and represented by mathematical equations as energy flow through an ecosystem. His conclusion, since corroborated for ecosystems across the planet beyond the field tests at Cedar Bog Lake, found that on average only 10 percent of energy consumed by organisms at one trophic level is transferred as biomass to the next. Essentially what Lindeman was talking about is a food chain. The scenario is handily represented in textbooks as a pyramid.

As seen in the graphic on the following page, organisms consume other organisms lower down on the food chain and in turn get consumed by those higher up. At the pyramid's base is the energy provided by the Sun. Above that are the primary producers—plants and algae—so-called autotrophs, or "self-feeders," who metabolize the Sun's energy through photosynthesis. The next level consists of heterotrophs, which feed directly on autotrophs. This category includes organisms ranging from large herbivores to microscopic bacteria. Carnivores—animals that eat other animals—and omnivores occupy the next level. Detritovores, or decomposers, which typically stand outside the pyramid but not outside the process, consume and recycle dead matter at all levels, putting some energy back into the system. The

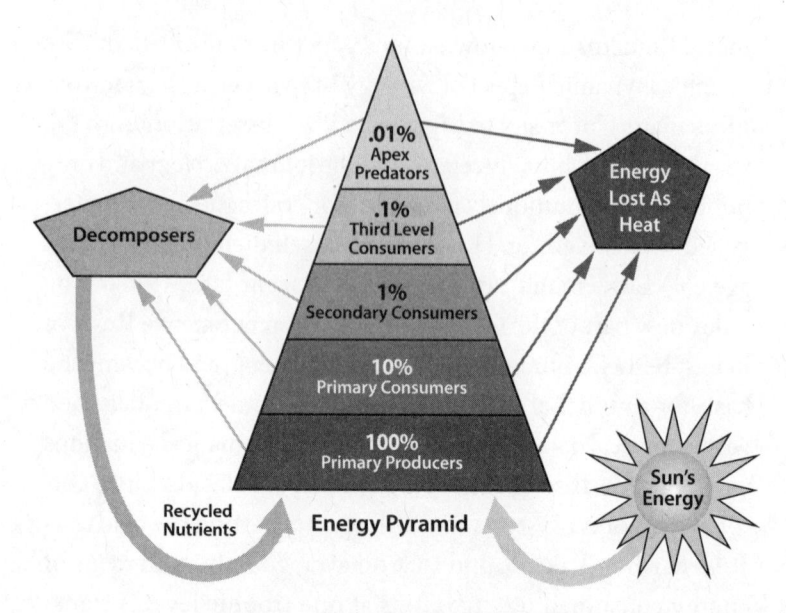

FIGURE 4.1. The Ecological Pyramid.

other 90 percent, however, thanks to the Second Law of Thermodynamics, is surplus energy, dissipated as waste heat.

Most people think of the modern human economy as based on money. But financial analyst Tim Morgan hits the bullseye and speaks for most ecological economists in the field today when he observes in *Life after Growth* (2013) that "ultimately, the economy is, and always has been, a surplus energy equation. As such, it is governed by the physical laws of thermodynamics, and not by the man-made 'laws' of the market." As for money itself, Morgan declares with the emphasis of italics that "*money is the language rather than the substance of the real economy*." The real economy to which Morgan refers and on which the market system feeds is an amalgam of energy, labor, and resources, the latter two of which items, one might notice, are themselves merely forms of energy.

"The real nature of money," Morgan observes further, "is that it forms a *claim* on the products of the real economy." The modern global financial system is thus wholly predicated on future returns and is catalyzed by debt. Indeed, one need not look very far to see how thoroughly leveraged governments, institutions, and individuals are worldwide. The federal debt of the United States, for example, stands at $32.52 trillion. American households add another $17 trillion. Moreover, since debt is a claim on future money, and money a claim ultimately on energy, this means that debt is a claim—or a gambler's bet—on the future availability and supply of energy. You can see immediately how tied we are to the welfare of Earth and its progenitor, the Sun, and how spending down Nature's capital reserves of energy, as we are doing, is profligate and self-destructive. It's like an entitled twenty-something blowing through his trust fund. The discovery of fossil fuels and the invention of the internal combustion engine has only accelerated the process by artificially dissociating us from the biophysical realities that make life possible in the first place.

But if that were not bad enough, the whole problem is compounded by the fact that most money in the modern global economy is created by commercial banks *ex nihilo*, that is, out of nothing, as might be expected from a regnant divinity. When a bank, for example, loans you money, it is not going down to its basement vaults and pulling out the requisite amount of cash it has on hand. It extends that sum as credit right there at the loan officer's desk based on the bank's accounting valuation—that is, its ledger value calculated on paper or on a spreadsheet—on the promise that you will pay it back with interest. What is more, it does not count the loan it just made to you as a deficit in its holdings, but as a new *asset*, meaning it has just created money out of thin air. And you, the loan recipient, can now go out and spend that newly minted money on goods and services that consume natural resources and produce by-products and pollutants that degrade and deplete existing stocks. Under such circumstances, it should be crystal clear to anyone paying attention how exponential growth gets its foothold. Banks are not intermediaries. They are agents of an artificial financial apparatus that operates independently of natural processes.

If you think I am overstating or misrepresenting this last point, you can hear it from the horse's mouth. Nobel laureate Robert Solow, for example, who developed the financial industry's standard model of growth, made the following astonishing claim in a lecture delivered in 1974: "The world can, in effect, get along without natural resources," Solow declared, cavalierly and specifically dismissive of the then newly published Club of Rome report *Limits to Growth*. "At some finite cost," he insists, "production can be freed of dependence on exhaustible resources altogether." Solow is a learned, theoretically attuned, and historically informed scholar, not a venal Wall Street trader. That he could arrive at such a demonstrably false conclusion, what the late ecological economist Herman Daly called a "recipe with no ingredients," is a symptom of our disease. Classicist Richard Seaford presents a historical thesis that explains in part how we got to this point. The invention of coined money, Seaford argues in *Money and the Early Greek Mind* (2004), with its unlimited nature and the symbolic sublimation it provides, gave rise to abstract thought, first in archaic Greece and India, and from there—a double-edged sword—accelerated a process of human alienation from biophysical constraints and from meaningful, productive social relations that had begun with the discovery of agriculture. But that angle is not entirely new. The harmful artificiality of money and the human and environmental costs of money-making occurred to the ancients themselves, their idea, paradoxically, a product of the abstract, philosophical thought that coinage spawned, a view coincident with its early proliferation.

Junk Bonds

Aristotle, for example, is just as exacting in his critique of money as Morgan. In discussing *oikonomia* ("house-management," whence *economy*) in the *Politics*, Aristotle says outright that money is merely a token and means of exchange, not an end in itself. It is, in fact, as he puts it, "worthless junk"—the word is *lēros* in Greek—"and wholly conventional. By nature," he says, "it is nothing." Proper economic management, he argues further, "takes more care for a household's human persons than for its inanimate goods." This last is an enlightened statement to which we will have occasion to return. But the real problem with the acquisition of wealth, according to Aristotle, is that money is, as Seaford elaborates in his study, *unlimited*—money making money based on nothing. This is what makes unearned income and usury so pernicious: "Its gain comes from money itself," Aristotle remarks,

and not from that for the sake of which money was invented. For money was brought into existence for the purpose of exchange, but interest increases the amount of the money itself; consequently, this form of the business of getting wealth is of all forms the most contrary to nature.

Accordingly, Aristotle recommends, unambiguously: "There should be a limit to all wealth."

The Greek word for "interest," *tokos*, literally means "offspring." It was by Aristotle's time a dead metaphor, yet drawn, paradoxically, from the language of biological reproduction, prompting Aristotle to etymologize it for us: "This is how the word arose," he says. "Things that are born," he observes, using its base verb *tiktō*, "resemble their parents; and so interest [*tokos*] is money born of money." We might imagine Aristotle fuming a bit beneath the surface of his text at the outrageousness of using a natural metaphor to describe what he regarded as an unnatural practice—unnatural, that is, because, in his view, self-increase and growth is not money's purpose. It is a means of exchange only. The ends of the exchange are the human persons on either side of a given transaction. Germano-Korean philosopher Byung-Chul Han, in a loosely Marxist analysis of the problem of freedom in a capitalist society, brings Aristotle's critique up to date for our era:

> Capital reproduces by entering into relations with itself as another form of Capital: through free competition. It copulates with the Other of itself by way of individual freedom. Capital grows inasmuch as people engage in free competition. Hereby, individual freedom amounts to servitude inasmuch as Capital lays hold of it and uses it for its own propagation. That is, Capital exploits individual freedom in order to breed. . . . In the process, individuals degrade into the genital organs of Capital.

The Cynic Demetrius, too, lends his voice to the chorus. When we last met Demetrius he was castigating the extraction industry of his age. He continues that same diatribe with words directed against the phantom systems of financial exchange: "Written certificates, IOUs, and contracts—what are these," he asks, "but empty images, devoid of real ownership, the shadowy bowers of Greed trying to work out a way to trick empty-headed people whose minds take pleasure in fantasies?"

> What are "profit," "an account book," and "interest" other than names made up for human greed that exceeds the bounds of Nature? I might complain that Nature didn't stash away her gold and silver more deeply within her, that she did not lay a heavier weight upon them, one that could not be dragged away, but what are these ledgers, these invoices, *time itself* for sale! And the bloodsucking 10 percent interest a month? They're evils sprung from our choices and our dispositions, that's what they are. There's nothing in them that can be held in the hand or placed before the eyes—dreams only, of empty Greed!

The idea that a moneylender is selling time, which belongs to no one except God, or the universe, is expressed by Demetrius here possibly for the first time in the historical record, yet it became a topos in later vituperations against usury. The Old Testament cadences of poet Ezra Pound (1885–1972) also underscore the point and are blunted only slightly by the author's unpoetic views on other matters. I say Old Testament not only with reference to Pound's verbal affectations, but also because usury is forbidden at Deuteronomy 23:19–20 and was outlawed by the Catholic Church up until the time of the Reformation. Yet the Aristotelian stamp of Pound's condemnation of usury as the usurper of human biological and creative fecundity is unmistakable. He calls it, unequivocally, "a sin against nature":

WITH USURA
wool comes not to market
sheep bringeth no gain with usura
Usura is a murrain, usura
blunteth the needle in the maid's hand
and stoppeth the spinner's cunning. Pietro Lombardo
came not by usura
Duccio came not by usura
nor Pier della Francesca; Zuan Bellin' not by usura
. . .
Usura rusteth the chisel
It rusteth the craft and the craftsman
It gnaweth the thread in the loom
. . .
Usura slayeth the child in the womb
It stayeth the young man's courting
It hath brought palsey to bed, lyeth
between the young bride and her bridegroom
    CONTRA NATURAM

Whatever we might think of Pound's screed, limits, we have seen, form the contours of sustainable systems. In today's globalized world, implementing limits on unnatural money-making will be essential if we are to retard, much less remediate, the environmental damage we are causing and to rectify gross sociopolitical asymmetries of access and power that have been exacerbated by the market economy. Economist Thomas Piketty and colleagues at the World Inequality Lab produced a report in 2022 that underscores the damaging effects of the global wealth gap in nearly every conceivable facet of human life. As Piketty summarized the report's key findings on Twitter (now X), "the richest 10% own around 60–80% of wealth in the various world regions. The poorest 50% always own less than 5%." Plotted on a graph, the rise in income inequality since World War II takes the shape of yet another hockey stick. The gap between rich and poor has not been so pronounced since the early twentieth century, the days of Standard Oil and Carnegie Steel. We live in a new Gilded Age.

What is more, the report says, public wealth—that is, public ownership of infrastructure such as schools and hospitals and of financial assets (less public debt)—stood at between 15 percent to 30 percent of total global wealth in the early 1980s. But that figure has dropped to "near 0% in most rich countries." In the United States, at least, the disparity between rich and poor wasn't always so steep. In the decades after World War II, the accumulation of wealth among the top 10 percent was impeded by progressive taxation. Between 1944 and 1981, for example, the top tax rate for the highest-earning Americans averaged 81 percent, compared with 37 percent today. Taxation, in other words, a limiting mechanism, redistributed money in the form of public goods and services. Lucas Chancel of the Paris School of Economics, co-director of the World Inequality Lab and lead author of its report, minces no words on the significance of this fact: "Inequality," he notes, "is always a political choice."

As the Trophic Pyramid illustrates, there will aways be surplus energy in Nature's systems, including in the secondary system of the human economy. What to do with it? Georges Bataille had some ideas.

Dépense

Aristotle argued that the proper use of surplus energy in the form of wealth is to cultivate friendships, get involved in one's community, and develop one's mind and one's spirit. He called these activities "leisure," *scholē* in Greek, whence our word "school." For Aristotle *scholē* is, as it were, a school of life—of living well; that is, philosophically—whose tuition is paid for by economic exchange. It is the end for which we work; money-making is but the limited means. *Scholē* includes rest and recreation, too, of course, but Aristotle is quick to emphasize that it is not "play," a word in Greek whose root implies childishness. He does not discount play altogether but views it as a kind of medicine or restorative tonic for a soul bent on higher things. In any event, all these activities, it will be seen, expend energy. In fact, one could argue they expend just as much or more energy than engaging in business.

Bataille's economic theory focuses precisely on this—expenditure (*dépense*)—the consumption of wealth, rather than its production. Summarizing the gist of the Trophic Pyramid without referring to it by name, Bataille explains how all living organisms consume more energy than they need to maintain life. That excess energy is used in part for growth, but "if the system can no longer grow, or if the excess cannot be completely absorbed in its growth," he observes, "it must necessarily be lost without profit." Surplus energy must be spent, he insists, "willingly or not, gloriously or catastrophically."

To illustrate his point Bataille uses the simple example of a calf. The moment it's birthed a calf begins expending energy to function as an independent organism. It nurses first from its mother, and then, eventually, shambles about to feed by itself on pasture, both of which activities contribute to its growth. If a farmer restricts or interferes with these natural behaviors, as happens in confinement agriculture, some excess energy is conserved on the animal as fat. A similar result is achieved if a male animal is castrated soon after birth, which is why beef sold at market are typically young steers. Castrated male animals are also more docile since they're not producing testosterone for reproduction and can thus be used more effectively as work animals, hence oxen.

When an animal reaches sexual maturity, some of its excess energy is diverted from its growth as an individual organism to reproduction and so the excess contributes to the increase, not of itself, but of the group. That, however, is all the growth a healthy calf will or can experience in its life, unless it's stricken with abnormal, cancerous growth of some kind. Yet its large adult body carries about only 10 percent of its total energy uptake over a lifetime. The rest is dissipated, as manure, for example. Now here is a point that Bataille does not make, because the science of his time had not flagged it, but it is in perfect keeping with his larger argument and serves as an instructive primer to the historical examples of *dépense* that he does discuss: As is well known now, ruminant digestion and manure release methane into the atmosphere, a harmful emission. The massive global uptick in human beef consumption over the past fifty years has made methane a major contributor to climate change. This is also well known. But it is a mistake to say, as the discourse surrounding this issue universally couches things, that *agriculture* is responsible for this harmful emission. It is not. *Eating* is the source of this problem. And one must eat. By 2050, ten billion of us must. One need not eat beef or other meat, of course, or one can eat less of it, but the arable land now used for growing grain and soy to feed beef and dairy cows would still need to be cultivated to replace meat in the diet with plant-based substitutes. The problem gets thornier when you consider that vast tracts of land currently grazed by animals are unsuitable for cultivation. Animals convert grass and scrub, which humans cannot eat, to sources of protein that we can.

Nor are plants themselves neutral in terms of impact. Continuous cultivation of arable land depletes nutrients in the soil, as we have seen, and lost nitrogen, potassium, and phosphates need regularly to be replenished. Currently that is done at large scale with synthetic fertilizers, whose processing requires large inputs of fossil fuels. Animal manure, by contrast, Nature's best fertilizer, is, at least in that respect, carbon neutral, resource conserving, and, as literally a waste product, cost-free. Animals, it becomes clear, have a role to play in the human food cycle and food system, and always have had. Happily, new technologies are helping to mitigate the negative impact of the large numbers of domesticated ruminants we now raise. Anaerobic manure digesters, for example, like the one at a large dairy farm down the road from us, can extract the methane in cow manure and use it to generate clean electricity. What is left behind is seasoned, ready-to-apply compost. The farm in question generates enough electricity, in fact, to power its whole operation, making it virtually self-sustaining. They call it cow power.

As Bataille emphasizes, it's not a question of *whether* excess energy must be dissipated, but *how* we choose to dissipate it. On this point he laments that "our ignorance . . . causes us to *undergo* what we could *bring about* in our own way, if we understood." The example of cows shows how Nature's system of generating surplus energy can work to our universal disadvantage (harmful emissions) or be harnessed for the greater good (compost and renewable electricity). Not to choose, however, or to choose unwisely; not to expend the surplus energy according to some plan or arrangement, consigns us to capricious, catastrophic destructions. War, for example, which Bataille interprets as the release of pressure built up by excessive growth in socioeconomic and political systems, is one of those outcomes. Specifically, he argues that the period of unprecedented industrialization in Europe from 1815 to 1914 led to surpluses that were discharged in World Wars I and II, both of which Bataille lived through and that form the existential backdrop to his work. "The greatest orgies of wealth," he calls them.

The rationale for this verdict applies to all technologically assisted growth: "Initially," Bataille observes, technologies "use a portion of the surplus energy, but then they produce a larger and larger surplus. This surplus eventually contributes to making growth more difficult, for growth no longer suffices to use it up." That analysis approximates the situation we currently face, where surplus that is not already directed toward further economic growth, as so much of it is—unnatural, "self-devouring" growth, as MacArthur genius grant recipient Julie Livingstone calls it—is exuded as pollution, as greenhouse gasses, as environmental and socioeconomic harm. What is more, Bataille points out, limits to all growth are fixed spatially by the biosphere itself; to exceed those limits will inevitably bring collapse. This is a remarkable observation for someone to make in this context in 1949. Bataille was way ahead of his time on this question.

Dépense is an anaerobic digester, as it were, for growth. Bataille's historical examples of *dépense* include instances of cultures that, like Europeans in World Wars I and II, expend surplus energy negatively via violence and bloodshed—the elaborate system of human sacrifice among the Aztecs, for example, and the sublimation of religious submission (*islam*) as military conquest in the nascent cultures of Islam. The potlatch feasts and extravagant gift-giving of the Tlingit, Haida, and Kwakiutl peoples in the Pacific Northwest, on the other hand, withdraw wealth from productive consumption, Bataille argues, following the work of compatriot Marcel Mauss (1872–1950), and expend it to reinforce instead social bonds of honor, rank, obligation, and emotional ties like respect, love, and gratitude. It is no wonder that American maverick economist Thorstein Veblen was also inspired by this Indigenous institution when he developed the notion of "conspicuous consumption" in his classic *Theory of the Leisure Class* (1899). (Although potlatch-like expenditure takes on a distinctly different character among robber barons and captains of industry.) Buddhism in Tibet, Bataille argues further, was the "radical solution" of *dépense* for a landlocked, resources-scarce, forbidding country that had "no other diversion." Large-scale exudations of Bataille's own time like Soviet-era industrialization and territorial expansion and its countermeasure, the US Marshall Plan of assistance to postwar Europe (1948–1951), also exemplify the paradigm, with mixed blessings.

The merits of Bataille's analyses need to be judged on a case-by-case basis; the evidence for some examples is more persuasive than for others. In every instance, however, Bataille was convinced that, should we care to look, we will find "solutions

FIGURE 4.2. Tlingit potlatch at Sitka, Alaska, 1904,
Haines Sheldon Museum.

to political problems deriving from traditional wisdom." "Ancient societies," he points out, "found relief in festivals; some erected admirable monuments that had no useful purpose." Whereas we moderns "use the excess to multiply 'services' that make life smoother." His remarks about the role of Buddhism in Tibet under the current Dalai Lama's predecessor—that is, before the Chinese invasion of 1950—are particularly astute, and sum up a key implication of his thesis:

> Totalitarian monasticism answers the need to stop the growth of a closed system. Just as Islam reserved all the excess for war, and the modern world for industrial development, Lamaism put everything into the contemplative life, the free play of the sensitive man in the world.... It ceases ... to subject life to any other ends but life itself: Directly and immediately, life is its own end.

Institutional monasticism, it will be readily observed, is extravagant expenditure and renunciation of expenditure at one and the same time. Seneca, who was not a monk, nonetheless argues along similar lines for indifference to material wealth, stating boldly, paradoxically, and with heavy irony (since he was perhaps the richest man in Rome in his time) that "it is a sign of a weak mind not to be able to endure riches." Wealth weighs us down, Seneca suggests, the surplus of it, and imposes a burden on life—ours, and the lives of others. It is a profound idea, practically a page out of Bataille, and shows that the contemplative life can clearly take many other forms than cenobitic monasticism.

Seneca's contemporary Philo of Alexandria (ca. 20 BCE– ca. 50 CE), for example, a Jewish scholar and theologian deeply influenced by Stoicism, describes the first fruits of *dépense* for those whose values align with Nature's ways. Commenting on the biblical Book of Numbers' elaborate prescriptions of daily offerings and sacrifices in the Temple, Philo declares that "every day is a festival for those who follow Nature and its laws." If we pursued virtuous living, Philo avers, "the time from birth to death would be one continuous festival. Houses and cities would rest in security and peace, full of all good things, and they would have fair weather in all their affairs." As it is, however, "men and women alike," Philo says, have succumbed to "over-reach," *pleonexia*, a Greek word that means literally having more than one's share. In the idiom of modern ecological economics, it would not be a stretch to translate it as "overshoot." We have, he says, "worked thereby against our own and others' interests by breaking the continuity of this joyful contentment." "Practitioners of wisdom," by contrast, Philo continues,

> be they Greeks or foreigners, who live blamelessly and without reproach, who refuse to do harm or retaliate with it, who avoid associating with busy-bodies and the places they frequent—law-courts, council-chambers, marketplaces—*their* zeal is for a peaceful life, free from war. They are fierce observers of Nature and all that it contains. Earth, sea, air, and heaven, and the creatures in them, are the objects of their research. . . . And while their bodies are firmly planted on solid ground, they fledge their souls with wings to cruise the upper air and contemplate the powers there, as befits true cosmopolitans—"citizens of the universe"—who realize that the world is a city, its citizens comrades in wisdom, enrolled on the register as such by Virtue, the vested president of this universal commonwealth.

Philo's lofty ideal links the personal and public spheres. A life lived according to Nature translates ethics into policies and social norms. Contemplation can inform our Constitutions. Research should underwrite our Republics. Indeed, Aristotle says outright in the *Politics* that "the student who is going to make a suitable investigation of the best form of government must necessarily decide first of all what is the most desirable mode of life."

In using the word "accursed" (*maudit*) in the title of his book, Bataille refers to the fact that in traditional, archaic societies whatever surplus is expended is usually deemed as sacred, consecrated, no-longer-ordinary. This dynamic is seen preeminently in sacrifice, as in the Book of Numbers, but evinced the world over: "Destruction," Bataille observes on this point, "is the best means of negating a utilitarian relation between man and the animal or plant." But he also means "accursed" in another, secular sense: "A curse obviously weighs on human life," he writes, "insofar as it does not have the strength to control a vertiginous movement. It must be stated as a principle, without hesitation, that the lifting of such a curse depends on man and *only on man*."

Bataille was not unaware of the difficulties involved in applying his ideas. As he confesses: "their implementation on the required scale is so difficult that from the outset the undertaking hardly looks encouraging." And yet, he insists, "the theoretical solution exists." At least one degrowth proponent has championed Bataille's notion of *dépense* with a view to reframing that movement's narrative: "Degrowth thought has to respond to the problem of abundance, not to scarcity. This means relearning how to waste, not how to reduce and recycle." We could expend economic surplus on so many fronts: free higher education for anyone who wants it, in both practical and purely theoretical or artistic pursuits; free public transportation, including interstate travel, fueled by renewables; extravagant support for scientific and humanistic research and the arts; lavish investment in sustainable, regenerative agriculture and a healthy food system; cost-free, total-coverage health care, including fitness center memberships and support for other activities for physical and mental well-being; and the big one: universal basic income, calibrated to regional costs of living—in a word, expenditure of surplus in support of all forms of *scholē* to facilitate a fulfilling life for everyone. We could do all of this. What else is life for? Denuclearization of the US military alone would free up $634 billion that the Departments of Energy and Defense plan to spend over the next twenty years (as reported by the Congressional Budget Office). It does not take much imagination to think of ways to put such waste to better use.

Disturbing Elements

When it comes to imagination, few other thinkers have had as much of it as John Ruskin. A staunch moralist with his fair share of Victorian-era flaws, Ruskin has been amply admired, but just as often parodied and pilloried. Emma Thompson's film *Effie Gray* (2014), for example, which is based on the titillating, historically true, yet thoroughly mysterious circumstances of Ruskin's unconsummated marriage to Euphemia Gray (who left him for painter John Everett Millais), depicts him as a cruel, domineering, impotent husband. In Mike Leigh's *Mr. Turner* (2014), starring Timothy Spall in the lead role, he is a feckless aesthete waving a hankie. (Ruskin was an early and vocal champion of J.M.W. Turner's painting and later executor of his estate.) Ruskin makes a cameo appearance in Tom Stoppard's play *The Invention of Love* (1997) as the avuncular curmudgeon everyone ignores. E. M. Forster had great fun putting Ruskin-esque sermons about Italian art on the lips of Reverend Cuth-bert Eager in *A Room with a View* (1908). The real Ruskin was, of course, not exactly any of these characters. To paraphrase Oscar Wilde, who was Ruskin's student at Oxford, caricature is perhaps the sincerest form of flattery that mediocrity can pay to greatness.

Indeed, it is an understatement to say that Ruskin's influence has been great. His ideas about art and artisanal skill seeded the Arts and Crafts and Pre-Raphaelite movements. A dogged advo-cate of architectural and landscape conservation, Ruskin is re-sponsible for what became the UK's National Trust and National Parks system. Academic institutions and museums are named after him, as is a town in Florida. His treatise *Unto This Last* in particular changed the course of many lives. British Prime Min-ister Clement Atlee (1883–1967), the first Labour candidate to hold that office in the challenging years immediately following World War II, declared of Ruskin's work, "It was through this gate that I entered the Socialist fold." Mohandas Gandhi (1869–1948) read *Unto This Last* in one sitting in 1904 on a twenty-four-hour train journey between Johannesburg and Durban, South Africa. In a chapter from his autobiography titled "The Magic Spell of a Book," Gandhi writes: "It gripped me"; "I could not get any sleep that night"; "I decided to change my life in accor-dance with the ideals of the book." And he did. Ruskin's ideas formed the basis of Gandhi's whole economic philosophy, called *Sarvodaya* ("welfare for all"), the title he gave to the paraphrase of *Unto This Last* that he published in his native Gujarati in 1908. Ruskin also undergirds the thinking behind Gandhi's declara-tions in *Hind Swaraj*, or "Indian Home Rule," published in 1909,

FIGURE 4.3. John Ruskin, *Self-portrait in Blue Neckcloth*, 1875.

banned by the British Raj as a seditious text, but which became the cornerstone of Indian independence.

Ruskin's life, work, and legacy are thus substantial, even if they are not unqualified triumphs. Ruskin himself in fact developed an aesthetic and worldview drawn from Nature that embraces human shortfalls and limitations. His thoughts on these matters contain within them also the germ of his most powerful economic idea. As he puts it in *The Stones of Venice* (1853), from a famous chapter titled "The Nature of Gothic,"

> Imperfection is in some sort essential to all that we know of life. It is the sign of life in a mortal body, that is to say, of a state of progress and change. Nothing that lives is, or can be, rigidly perfect; part of it is decaying, part nascent. The foxglove blossom,—a third part bud, a third part past, a third part in full bloom,—is a type of the life of this world. And in all things that live there are certain irregularities and deficiencies which are not only signs of life, but sources of beauty. All admit irregularity as they imply change; and to banish imperfection is to destroy expression, to check exertion, to paralyse vitality.

Life and vitality, Ruskin argues in *Unto This Last*, echoing Aristotle, are the beating heart of human economic exchange. Or at least they should be.

———

Ruskin begins *Unto This Last* with the Dickensian image of a starving mother, her children, and a crust of bread. His point of departure is a recent workers' strike that the then-new, self-proclaimed "science" of political economy touted by David Ricardo in *The Principles of Political Economy and Taxation* (1817) and John Stuart Mill in *Principles of Political Economy* (1848), Ruskin insists, is powerless to resolve, much less comprehend. Market logic proceeds by a calculation wherein what Ruskin calls the social affections are "accidental and disturbing elements in human nature," whereas acquisitiveness and a desire for progress are the constant ones. "Let us eliminate the inconstants," Ruskin imagines his economist opponent to say, "and, considering the human being merely as a covetous machine, examine by what laws of labour, purchase, and sale, the greatest accumulative result in wealth is obtainable." But human relationships, Ruskin points out, don't work according to this calculus. "The disturbing elements in the social problem," he notes, "are not of the same nature as the constant ones: they alter the essence of the creature under examination the moment they are added; they operate, not mathematically, but chemically."

The social problem of a workers' strike consists in the relationship between an employer and the employed, "the first vital problem that political economy has to deal with." Market economics pronounces the impasse of a strike to be a clash of interests that produces an antagonism between the two parties. But the mother and her crust introduce a disturbing element that changes that equation. "If there is only a crust of bread in the house," Ruskin observes,

> and mother and children are starving, their interests are not the same. If the mother eats it, the children want it; if the children eat it, the mother must go hungry to her work. Yet is does not necessarily follow that there will be "antagonism" between them, that they will fight for the crust, and that the mother, being the strongest, will get it, and eat it.

"Neither in any other case," Ruskin concludes, "whatever the relations of the persons may be, can it be assumed for certain that, because their interests are diverse, they must necessarily regard each other with hostility." Ostensibly concerned in *Unto*

This Last with the relationship of employers and workers in Industrial Age England, the thrust of Ruskin's larger argument is that, by nature and convention, human communities at their best, at other times and other places, have weighed their net worth not by the "balance of expediency," as market laws would have it, but by the "balances of justice."

For Ruskin the justice involved between employer and the employed is evinced primarily in wages for labor. As far as affections are concerned, the relationship between worker and employer in a competitive, market economy, he argues, tends toward *dis*affection because wages fluctuate and undercompensate for the goods or services rendered. The title of Ruskin's treatise reflects this phenomenon, still very much with us. It refers to the biblical Parable of the Workers in the Vineyard in the Gospel of Matthew. A good householder, the parable relates, hires workers in the morning to labor in his vineyard for the agreed price of a penny; additional workers join the crew at midday at the same rate, and more still in the afternoon. At the eleventh hour, the householder hires one more. When wages are paid at the end of the day, each worker receives the same agreed upon amount. The workers hired in the morning, however, complain that they should be paid more than those hired later since they bore "the burden and heat of the day." But the householder replies, "Friend, I do thee no wrong: didst not thou agree with me for a penny? Take what is thine and go thy way: I will give unto this last, even as unto thee."

Its eschatological meaning aside (the kingdom of heaven is somehow like this, the Gospel says), the parable underscores Ruskin's practical recommendation that workers who do the same job should be paid the same wage. The rate of that wage in Ruskin's proposed scheme would be tied to the difficulty and amount of skill and education required to do the work, the quality of which would be its own reward—to both the worker and employer: Bad work would be self-selected out of the system, and people who do good work would never face market pressure to charge less for their labor to undercut the competition. Throughout his life Ruskin was adamant on this last point. In "The Work of Iron, in Nature, Art, Policy," for example, an invited lecture delivered at Tunbridge Wells, a town in Kent known for its iron-rich natural springs (hence the subject of his talk), in 1858, Ruskin declares

> Whenever we buy, or try to buy, cheap goods—goods offered at a price which we know cannot be remunerative for the labour involved in them. . . . Whenever we buy such goods, remember we are stealing somebody's labour. Don't let us mince the matter. I say, in plain Saxon, STEALING—taking from him the proper reward of his work, and putting it into our own pocket.

Similarly, when invited by the city fathers of Bradford, a bustling commercial hub made prosperous by the woolen textile industry, to offer architectural advice for building a new Exchange in 1864, Ruskin gave them more than they bargained for. His remarks, in a lecture he called "Traffic," bear quoting at length for their sheer impertinence and their clear preference for ancient ways and means:

> Your Greek worshipped Wisdom, and built you the Parthenon—the Virgin's temple. The Mediæval worshipped Consolation, and built you Virgin temples also—but to our Lady

of Salvation. Then the Revivalist worshipped beauty, of a sort, and built you Versailles, and the Vatican. Now, lastly, will you tell me what *we* worship, and what *we* build?

Now, we have, indeed, a nominal religion, to which we pay tithes of property, and sevenths of time; but we have also a practical and earnest religion, to which we devote nine-tenths of our property and six-sevenths of our time. And we dispute a great deal about the nominal religion; but we are all unanimous about this practical one, of which I think you will admit that the ruling goddess may be best generally described as the "Goddess of Getting-on," or "Britannia of the Market." The Athenians had an "Athena Agoraia," or Minerva of the Market: but she was a subordinate type of their goddess, while our Britannia Agoraia is the principal type of ours. And all your great architectural works, are, of course, built to her. It is long since you built a great cathedral; and how you would laugh at me, if I proposed building a cathedral on the top of one of these hills of yours, taking it for an Acropolis! But your railroad mounds, prolonged masses of Acropolis; your railroad stations, vaster than the Parthenon, and innumerable; your chimneys, how much more mighty and costly than cathedral spires! Your harbour-piers; your warehouses; your exchanges!—all these are built to your great Goddess of "Getting-on;" and she has formed, and will continue to form, your architecture, as long as you worship her; and it is quite vain to ask me to tell you how to build to *her*; you know far better than I.

A concern for justice—the regulating constant in human affairs—permeates the whole of Ruskin's vision for a healthy political economy, even where it is not the explicit focus of discussion in any given instance. The title of the third of the four essays that make up *Unto This Last*, for example, is "Qui Judicatis Terram." Its Latin phrase, the first words of the Vulgate *Wisdom of Solomon* (an authoritative part of the Roman Catholic canon of scripture, part of the Protestant "Apocrypha"), means "You who judge the earth," meaning those in power. But the resonant core of the thought is the unquoted command in the first half of the title's original sentence, alluded to later in the essay, *Diligite iustitiam*—"*Love justice.*" Ruskin was raised a staunch Evangelical, even though he himself experienced what he calls a distinct "unconversion" while visiting Turin in 1858. It is no surprise, then, that *Unto This Last* is suffused with biblical quotations and allusions, some of them rather obscure, even for the *cognoscenti*. But Ruskin's classical influences run as deep or deeper, as his remarks in the lecture hall at Tunbridge Wells make clear. If their extent has not been as fully appreciated, perhaps that is because his classics intermingle so seamlessly with passages from Old and New Testament greats. Nonetheless, as he declares openly in his preface to *Unto This Last*, the definition of wealth that he will proceed to elaborate in his treatise "for the first time in plain English," he says, what he calls "the real gist of these papers," "has often been incidentally given in good Greek by Plato and Xenophon, and good Latin by Cicero and Horace." Above all, his predilection for economy's etymological and conceptual roots— the "house-law" (*oikonomia*) of Aristotle and Xenophon and those authors' prioritizing of the household's persons over its material goods—form the backbone of his thinking.

In his relentless pursuit of justice Ruskin is perhaps following Plato and his *Republic* most closely of all. The affiliation is captured perfectly in Ruskin's conclusion that

The whole question, therefore, respecting not only the advantage, but even the quantity of national wealth, resolves itself finally into one of abstract justice. It is impossible to conclude, of any given mass of acquired wealth, merely by the fact of its existence, whether it signifies good or evil to the nation in the midst of which it exists. Its real value depends on the moral sign attached to it.

Ruskin illustrates what he means with a parable of his own, in his telling far better than this mere summary here. Two sailors are cast away on an uninhabited coast. At first they farm the land of the interior in common and prosper. Over time they decide, out of no enmity, to divide the land into equal shares, and prosper still, each to his own, until one of them falls ill. Naturally the sick man will ask his friend to help him sow and harvest. The healthy man, "with perfect justice," Ruskin says, might ask for a written promise stating that his sick friend will give equal hours of labor in return, when he recovers, to compensate him for loss due to time away from work at his own farm. This arrangement persists for several years. Both properties, Ruskin observes, and both men will have suffered loss, the healthy man unable to devote full time to his own affairs, and the sick man the same, now indebted on top of that for several years' worth of labor to the other. "Considered as a 'Polis,' or state," Ruskin writes, "they will be poorer than they would have been otherwise . . . and the relations in which they stand to each other are also widely altered."

Add a third man into the mix, Ruskin observes, and the outcome becomes worse: The division of land is into thirds; each man specializes in a certain kind of produce to maximize his comparative advantage; to administer the transfer of goods from one farm to the other one of them agrees to be a superintendent in exchange for some remunerative share of the goods conveyed; soon this middle man sees his own comparative advantage of hoarding goods to create scarcity, "ingeniously watching his opportunities to possess himself regularly of the greater part of the superfluous produce of the two estates." The result, as Ruskin notes, is mercantile wealth, and, as in the parable of the two castaways "the wealth of the State, or of the three men considered as a society, is collectively less than it would have been had the merchant been content with juster profit. The operations of the two agriculturalists have been cramped to the utmost," he explains,

> and the continual limitations of the supply of things they wanted at critical times, together with the failure of courage consequent on the prolongation of a struggle for mere existence, without any sense of permanent gain, must have seriously diminished the effective results of their labour; and the stores finally accumulated in the merchant's hands will not in any wise be of equivalent value to those which, had his dealings been honest, would have filled at once the granaries of the farmers and his own.

The view of justice in a mercantile economy that Ruskin ultimately adopts is surprisingly akin to one propounded by its first advocate, the Greek poet Hesiod (ca. 750 BCE), who deeply influenced Plato's thinking, too. "Political economy," Ruskin writes, "(the economy of a State, or of citizens) consists simply in the production, preservation, and distribution, at fittest time and place, of useful or pleasurable things."

The farmer who cuts his hay at the right time; the ship-wright who drives his bolts well home in sound wood; the builder who lays good bricks in well-tempered mortar; the housewife who takes care of her furniture in the parlour, and guards against all waste in her kitchen; and the singer who rightly disciplines, and never overstrains her voice, are all political economists in the true and final sense: adding continually to the riches and well-being of the nation to which they belong.

This assessment is over 2,500 years and yet a mere stone's throw away from Hesiod's excellent advice from the *Works and Days*. As Ruskin quotes that poem elsewhere in *Unto This Last*—in Greek, no less—there's no doubt that he'd been reading the bard from Boeotia. In a mercantile context, cautioning his audience not to overload a ship, lest it sink, or a wagon, lest its axle break, Hesiod declares:

> Do not put all your provisions in hollow boats.
> Load the lesser part and leave the bulk aside,
> for it's a disaster to meet with grief on the waves at sea.
> Awful, too, if by hoisting excess weight onto your wagon
> you wreck its axle and the cargo is ruined.
> Observe measures; rightness is best in all things.

The word *kairos* in Greek, translated earlier as "rightness," is virtually a gloss on the preceding word in the first half of that line, "measures" (*metra*). The word is drawn from the vocabulary of archery and weaving. In ancient archery *kairos* referred to a vulnerable aperture in a target at which one aimed, like a "bullseye," or a "chink" in armor. In weaving it denoted the triangular opening where a weaver sent the woof-thread (attached to a shuttle) through the warp (not unlike English "loophole"). From these original uses the word came to mean doing something skillfully, with precision, at just the right moment. The word I translate as "provisions" earlier literally means "life" (*bios*), as in the *means* of life; the adjective "excess" is *hyperbios*, which the dictionaries will tell you derives from the Greek noun *biē*, "force/strength," but, coming hard on the heels of *bios*, and in the hands of a resourceful poet like Hesiod who was always keen on folk etymologies, suggests "beyond (*hyper*) what life (*bios*) requires," or, perhaps not unfairly in this context, "surplus." Even if that were true, did Ruskin know any of this? There's no way to tell, but it doesn't matter, as his equation of wealth and trade with life, about which more later, and his call to observe the just times and seasons of good measure put him squarely in Hesiod's camp.

In looking around at the professions of his own day Ruskin asks what characterizes each one—lawyer, physician, clergyman, soldier—and concludes that it is self-sacrifice that both binds them together and sets them apart as "so-called liberal professions." "The soldier's trade," for example, in offering his life in service to his country, "verily and essentially, is not slaying but being slain." The physician's is to die rather than leave his post in a plague. A merchant, by contrast, is, in the popular imagination, "presumed to act always selfishly. His work may be very necessary to the community; but the motive of it is understood to be wholly personal." Against this too-often accurate stereotype Ruskin proposes that, in a market economy with increasing need of merchants, "in true commerce, as in true preaching, or true fighting, it is necessary to admit the idea of occasional voluntary loss" that sixpences have to be lost, as well as lives, under a sense of duty; that the market may have its martyrdoms as well as the pulpit; and trade its heroisms as well as war.

The merchant's function, in short, is to provide and distribute goods to a nation for the welfare of all. Ruskin goes on to say some very remarkable things on this topic, to which we will return shortly, after considering this important question: What constitutes distribution in a market economy? What are its operations?

Science and Nescience

Midway through *Unto This Last*, Ruskin, always keen on pictures drawn from Nature, develops an extended metaphor of a river, "the flowing of streams to the sea," to describe the just action of wealth in society. He then turns the same image, cheekily, against "the popular economist" who believes that the market, left to its own devices, operates by some natural law, like the physical laws that govern the flow of rivers, namely, "that where demand is, supply must follow." To the contrary, Ruskin observes, the course of rivers can be controlled by human forethought and intervention. "Whether the stream shall be a curse or a blessing," he writes, "depends upon man's labour, and administering intelligence."

The idea that markets, like rivers, are self-organizing and best left to their own devices, or best left alone, already a feature of orthodox economic thinking in Ruskin's time, has become a new orthodoxy, thanks to the administering intelligence of F. A. Hayek (1899–1992). Hayek, an economist of the so-called Chicago School and a pioneer complexity theorist, argued that wide distribution of and ready access to knowledge and information is the precondition and distinguishing mark of prosperous societies. In an influential essay titled "The Use of Knowledge in Society" (1945), a market economy, Hayek suggested, is a dispersal system for knowledge and information. Conversely, he argued, social institutions, like markets, are themselves self-organizing epistemic devices. He articulates the essence of his position in several places in this paper, but here is as good a statement as any:

> The economic problem of society is . . . not merely a problem of how to allocate "given" resources—if "given" is taken to mean given to a single mind which deliberately solves the problem set by these "data." It is rather a problem of how to secure the best use of resources known to any of the members of society, for ends whose relative importance only these individuals know. Or, to put it briefly, it is a problem of the utilization of knowledge which is not given to anyone in its totality.

No one person or entity, to put it in layperson's terms, knows what the best use of anything is and should thus refrain from suggesting, much less imposing, it. In "The Theory of Complex Phenomena" (1964), Hayek theorized further in this same vein that conditions in social and political life that are conducive to freedom are identical with patterns of interaction that arise in the market. Political and hence personal freedom, in other words, are a function of economic freedom. In the United States this idea has been reinforced structurally twice over by the Supreme Court in major decisions, first in its determination that a corporation possesses all the rights and privileges, juridically speaking, of a human person, even though its individual shareholders bear none of the responsibilities, duties, obligations, or liabilities that result from corporate actions, which might appear a troubling verdict against jurisprudence in the eyes of those who recall US history, that the "equal protection under the laws" guaranteed to persons by the Fourteenth Amendment, ratified in 1868, originated with the abolition of slavery. A second, related stroke was *Citizens United v. FEC* (2010), which made financial contributions to political campaigns the equivalent of free speech, protected under the First Amendment.

In *The Road to Serfdom* (1944), his best-known work, Hayek warns against the negative flip side of his thesis: Top-down intervention, planning, or control by government destroys this self-regulating system and the freedom and prosperity that are said to be its emergent properties. Intervention, he argues, leads inevitably to totalitarianism. Despite the fact that Hayek himself actually penned a manifesto titled "Why I Am Not a Conservative" (1960) and dedicated *The Road to Serfdom* to "Socialists of All Parties," his socioeconomic ideas and their perceived political implications have sometimes made him a figurehead nonetheless for conservative and libertarian causes.

Ruskin, who described himself as at one and the same time "the reddest of the red," "a Communist of the old school," and "a violent Tory of the old school" (and who was most certainly the latter, officially), saw things differently. Hayek employed a Greek word to describe the workings of his theory: *catallaxy* ("exchange"), which he defines as "the order brought about by the mutual adjustment of many individual economies in a market." Ruskin, plying his typical wordplay, dismissed catallactics, the would-be "Science of Exchange," in 1862, using that word in *Unto This Last*, long before and unbeknownst to Hayek, as "a science founded on nescience" whenever the exchange disadvantages a weaker party. As he explains, with apt sarcasm:

> If I can exchange a needle with a savage for a diamond, my power of doing so depends either on the savage's ignorance of social arrangements in Europe, or on his want of power to take advantage of them, by selling the diamond to anyone else for more needles. If, farther, I make the bargain as completely advantageous to myself as possible, by giving to the savage a needle with no eye in it (reaching, thus, a sufficiently satisfactory type of the perfect operation of catallactic science), the advantage to me in the entire transaction depends wholly upon the ignorance, powerlessness, or heedlessness of the person dealt with. Do away with these, and catallactic advantage becomes impossible. So far, therefore, as the science of exchange relates to the advantage of one of the exchanging persons only, it is founded on the ignorance or incapacity of the opposite person. Where these vanish, it also vanishes.

This stunningly insightful scenario captures simultaneously the historical fact that the rise of capitalism in Europe was coeval with exactly the kind of colonial encounters that Ruskin describes and, with remarkable prescience, the flaw in Hayek's theory. Take away ignorance and incapacity, as Ruskin advises, and the outcomes of exchange become just and fair. The philosophical commonplace that knowledge is power thus takes on a new meaning in Ruskin's political economy. In the same passage where he recommends making a necessity of the virtue of voluntary loss in commerce, Ruskin observes:

Because the production or obtaining of any commodity involves necessarily the agency of many lives and hands, the merchant becomes in the course of his business the master and governor of large masses of men in a more direct, though less confessed way, than a military officer or pastor; so that on him falls, in great part, the responsibility for the kind of life they lead: and it becomes his duty, not only to be always considering how to produce what he sells, in the purest and cheapest forms, but how to make the various employments involved in the production, or transference of it, most beneficial to the men employed.

"The universal and constant action of justice in this matter," he reasons, "is therefore to diminish the power of wealth, in the hands of one individual, over masses of men, and to distribute it through a chain of men." The result? "To diminish the power of wealth, first, in acquisition of luxury, and secondly, in exercise of moral influence." Aristotle, or any other ancient philosopher, for that matter, might have agreed.

Hayek seemed unaware of or unwilling to entertain the idea espoused by many ecological economists today that markets can use price signals to bring capital under some measure of shared, social control that falls far short of "totalitarianism." Carbon taxes, for example, or tariffs on goods produced by exploited labor, which have been proposed as deterrents to the kinds of harm wrought in free markets, are themselves in fact a form of the dissemination of knowledge in society, an information signal about its values and priorities. But the larger issue at stake is not primarily economic, but ethical, and ecological: *In a world of finite resources free markets will eventually make conditions conducive to freedom impossible.* Everything returns to where it all began, and on which all things depend, which is our destiny, too: sovereign Nature.

Hayek opposed the social control of capital. He opposed, in short, *socialism*, having experienced, as an Austrian émigré to Britain and later the United States, its worst forms leading up to, during, and after World War II. But concentrated capital, as Ruskin realized in his own time, is already under antisocial control by monopolistic and oligopolistic power. Corporations engage in strategic planning and political lobbying to reduce market uncertainty, to secure favorable tax rates and deregulation, and to minimize their liability for externalities inflicted on common-pool resources like fresh water, air, land, and sea, and ecosystem services like, well, free access to knowledge and information. What is worse, the current regime of social media and Big Data has transformed the disciplinary power of biopolitics that Foucault was such a keen observer of, turning it into what Byung-Chul Han calls the "smart power" of *psychopolitics*, which "cosies up to the psyche rather than disciplining it through coercion and prohibitions." What Han describes is a form of phishing and focus grouping:

> It does not impose silence. Rather, it is constantly calling on us to confide, share, and participate: to communicate our opinions, needs, wishes, and preferences—to tell all about our lives.

Han brings the interplay of knowledge, power, and moral compass alarmingly up to date when he observes of our own time that

Smart power with a liberal, friendly appearance—power that stimulates and seduces—is more compelling than power that imposes, threatens, and decrees. Its signal and seal is the *Like* button. Now, people subjugate themselves to domination by consuming and communicating—and they click *Like* all the while. Neoliberalism is the *capitalism of "Like."* It is fundamentally different from nineteenth-century capitalism, which operated by means of disciplinary constraints and prohibitions.

Smart power reads and appraises our conscious and unconscious thoughts. It places its stock in voluntary self-organization and self-optimization. As such, it has no need to overcome resistance. Mastery of this sort requires no great expenditure of energy or violence. It simply *happens*.

The capitalism of *Like* should come with a warning label: *Protect me from what I want.*

Here, too, Ruskin, for all his Victorian trappings, was far ahead of his time. In his admonitions to the kingpins of Bradford, Ruskin, the art critic, turns this problem on its head where it belongs: "Taste is not only a part and an index of morality;—it is the ONLY morality. The first, and last, and closest trial question to any living creature is, 'What do you like?' Tell me what you like, and I'll tell you what you are."

Protect me from what I want.

"These Are My Jewels"

"Since the essence of wealth consists in power over men, will it not follow," Ruskin asks in the final essay of *Unto This Last*, "that the nobler and the more in number the persons are over whom it has power, the greater the wealth? Perhaps it may even appear, after some consideration, that the persons themselves *are* the wealth."

To support this claim Ruskin turns once again to antiquity, and a story preserved by Valerius Maximus (fl. 14–37 CE) about Cornelia, the mother of the brothers Gracchi, Gaius (ca. 154–121 BCE) and Tiberius (ca. 163–133 BCE). Cornelia, Valerius recounts, was entertaining a fellow mother from Campania as a guest in her house. The Campanian matron was quite keen to show off her jewelry, the finest work on offer at that time. Cornelia kept her engaged in conversation about her bijoux until her children—young Tiberius and Gaius—returned from school, whereupon she declared in turn, "These are *my* jewels."

It is an interesting choice of anecdote, invoked briefly to exemplify Ruskin's view that "the true veins of wealth are purple,—and not in Rock, but in Flesh—perhaps even that the final outcome and consummation of all wealth is in the producing as many as possible full-breathed, bright-eyed, and happy-hearted human creatures." The Gracchi became martyrs for the cause of economic and social reform and were lionized as such in ancient Rome. Tiberius, as tribune of the plebs, championed a comprehensive bill in 133 BCE designed to enforce a centuries-old law limiting landholding by individual Roman citizens. Its purpose was to break up large estates, *latifundia* (essentially factory farms), and redistribute land to the growing number of landless poor and veterans, who had found themselves displaced and were migrating to the overpopulated metropolis. For his efforts Tiberius was assassinated by senatorial elites. Gaius, who took up his brother's reformist mantle, also paid for it with his life.

Doubtless, these details were not lost on Ruskin, who perhaps means his readers to recall the Gracchi's valorous politics of fair distribution.

This final essay is in fact titled "Ad Valorem." It contains an inquiry into what constitutes value. Ruskin's conclusion is that "the value of a thing is independent of opinion, and of quantity. Think what you will of it, gain how much you may of it, the value of the thing itself is neither greater nor less." To drive his point home and to debunk the card-carrying economist's notion (in this case Mill's) that value is simply something's market worth in exchange, Ruskin summons up the classics once again, this time with both irony and indignation:

> Much store has been set for centuries upon the use of our English classical education. It were to be wished that our well-educated merchants recalled to mind always this much of their Latin schooling,—that the nominative of *valorem* (a word already sufficiently familiar to them) is *valor*; a word which, therefore, ought to be familiar to them. *Valor*, from *valēre*, to be well or strong (ὑγιαίνω);—strong, *in* life (if a man), or valiant; strong, *for* life (if a thing), or valuable. To be "valuable," therefore, is to "avail towards life." A truly valuable or availing thing is that which leads to life with its whole strength. In proportion as it does not lead to life, or as its strength is broken, it is less valuable; in proportion as it leads away from life, it is unvaluable or malignant.

Ruskin's ultimate verdict on the question of value becomes a solemn inscription, printed by him in Roman capitals as if it were a decree of the SPQR, or perhaps, in anticipation, an epitaph for market capitalism:

There is no Wealth but Life.

———

Ruskin's engagement with the classics is not perfunctory or a stylistic affectation. Rather it represents a creative upcycling of the past to address contemporary concerns. Ruskin, himself a resourceful artist of considerable talent, scours the scrap heap of history to construct a newly useful and morally beautiful economic worldview out of found objects from antiquity. What I find so admirable about Ruskin's work is that it is rooted in ancient modes of thought yet was fertilized and brought to fruition by issues and controversies of his own time. His ability to translate traditional thought and values for a changed and changing world makes him, I think, perennially relevant.

Does he, or Bataille, pass the sniff test for modern Academe? Probably not. Both were oddball mavericks in their day and remain so now. Bataille argued that the function of a human economy, following Nature's economy, is to spend. Ruskin anticipates this idea in his own way when he says, just prior to his proclamation that wealth is nothing more or less than life,

> The manner and issue of consumption . . . are the real tests of production. Production does not consist in things laboriously made, but in things serviceably consumable; and the question for the nation is not how much labour it employs, but how much life it produces.

To which he adds: "The prosperity of any nation is in exact proportion to the quantity of labour which it spends in obtaining and employing the means of life . . . not merely wisely producing, but wisely distributing and consuming." "Wise consumption," Ruskin ventures, "is a far more difficult art than wise production."

When Thoreau, who died the year *Unto This Last* was published, discusses housebuilding in the very first chapter of *Walden*, titled, appropriately, "Economy," he makes, as we have seen, the perceptive assertion that "the cost of a thing is the amount of what I will call life which is required to be exchanged for it, immediately or in the long run." Contrary to the popular maxim, time is not money. The notion that it is could only have occurred to someone beholden, actually or aspirationally, to a market economy. We are all of course beholden, but time, like wealth, is really life, the most precious commodity we can possess, which cannot be bought or sold or saved, only spent and consumed, wisely or unwisely. The one certainty we all face, the one maxim that remains always true, is that time is running out. That's its nature. Ruskin and Bataille invite us to make the best of it for the good of all.

Are their ideas utopian? I have provided ample room throughout to let Ruskin speak for himself. On this topic, too, I give him the last word, from the second of two "Lectures on Painting and Architecture" delivered in Edinburgh in 1853:

> Utopianism: that is another of the devil's pet words. I believe the quiet admission which we are all of us so ready to make that, because things have long been wrong, it is impossible they should ever be right, is one of the most fatal sources of misery and crime from which this world suffers. Whenever you hear a man dissuading you from attempting to do well, on

FIGURE 4.4. John Ruskin's personal seal
and motto "To-day."

the ground that perfection is "Utopian," beware of that man. Cast the word out of your dictionary altogether. There is no need for it. Things are either possible or impossible—you can easily determine which, in any given state of human science. If the thing is impossible, you need not trouble yourselves about it; if possible, try for it. . . . Utopianism is not our business—the *work* is.

Taking Stock: An Epilogue

IT'S TIME to take stock.

It's an interesting phrase, that, first attested in 1736 to indicate drawing up an inventory of goods, coming eventually to mean to think carefully about something before deciding what to do next. The related phrase *to take stock in*, on the other hand, is an expression of confidence, "to regard something as important," a usage dating from 1870 or so and emanating from the world of financial investment and capital gains. Both idioms arose because sheep, goats, and cows were once as good as gold—*livestock*—and in some parts of the world they still are. The Roman antiquarian Pliny the Elder (23–79 CE), at any rate, expresses delight that the Latin word for money, *pecunia*, was derived from *pecus* ("a flock or herd animal") and that fines in his day were still levied at the market price of oxen and sheep.

Originally, however, the word *stock*, of Germanic origin, denoted a stump or stick (*Stück*), the lifeless mass that's left behind once you've chopped down a tree—*dead*stock you might say. In recommending that we look again to the past to learn to live in the present and future, following Nature's lead,

I only hope not to have become a *laughingstock*, a compound derived from this original sense as a useless remainder, worthy only of scorn, a stick in the mud, as it were.

And yet anyone who has cut down a deciduous tree will know that it soon grows back. (Conifers, alas, tend not to.) Hence the idea of coming from good stock, meaning that one's root system and potential for life is strong and vigorous. This bundle of associative meanings and images pretty much sums up my stab at a conclusion here. Let's take stock of the various arguments we've collected, consider whether they come from good stock, and whether they're something we should take stock in. Are they livestock or deadstock?

There are many potential objections to any argument and, these days, it seems, doubt about what constitutes facts and evidence itself. What is worse, whataboutery, which characterizes so much public discourse, has trickled up, even to Academe. What about ancient slavery and chauvinism? Didn't Aristotle argue that slavery was "natural"? Didn't he think that women were biologically inferior, defective versions of men? Weren't all the ancient elites whose writings survive ultimately colonizers and oppressors?

Whiggery, too—the idea that humans in the present categorically know better than humans in the past—is another obstacle. Scientifically, the ancients were flat wrong about all sorts of things. Look no further for proof of our superiority, believers in progress say, than all the conveniences and improvements wrought by the applied science of technology. We risk anachronism and distortion if we use modern frameworks and concepts to describe ancient adumbrations of later discoveries. Leave the past as it was. We should not read it in the light of present concerns.

I would argue to the contrary that we cannot but read the past with eyes on the present. The past is not some fixed and static entity, stretched out conveniently like a corpse on the examination table to be dissected and studied in a hermetically sealed chamber. Indeed, Herbert Butterfield, the constitutional historian who gave us the phrase "whig interpretation of history" in 1931, himself believed that "we are all of us exultant and unrepentant whigs," and described his discipline not as the study of origins, but as "the analysis of all the mediations by which the past was turned into our present."

The mediations of our immediate past have yielded a paradigm that sees Nature as a mechanism, a machine even, whose levers we humans can pull to produce outputs that we like or think advantageous. The machine paradigm is founded on a reductive approach to scientific inquiry—a focus on working parts at the expense of emergent wholes. Reductionism, however, is not a bogey man, as it's often presented in some circles. It's how hard science works—to reduce a problem or object of investigation to its simplest form by analysis and experiment— and it has produced impressive results. It has a role to play in any worldview.

The problem is that the mechanistic approach is fundamentally an anthropocentric one, where, in the words of an old sophist, Protagoras of Abdera (485–415 BCE), "the *anthropos* is the measure of all things." Anthropocentrism and its benevolent corollary, old-fashioned humanism, has produced some good results, too, first and foremost the gradual recognition and protection of human dignity and human rights. In fact, Butterfield got his phrase from a tendency among early practitioners of English constitutional history, who belonged politically to the

Whig party, to see the broadening of human rights as a realization, in the fullness of time, of feeble gropings in the past.

The trouble with anthropocentrism, though, is that it has also created the Anthropocene. We now live in an age where human-induced harm is arguably greater in aggregate than human-produced good, threatening to make the planet unlivable not only for us, but for other species, too. This is also the conclusion reached by Swiss philosopher Dominique Bourg and his colleague Sophie Swaton, a philosophically inclined economist, in their magnificent book *Primauté du vivant* (2021), whose title, "Primacy of Life," a play on the French legal phrase for the "rule of law" (*primauté du droit*), recalls Ruskin, and whose subtitle, "An Essay on What Is Thinkable" (*Essai sur le pensable*), points to the possibilities of a way forward. Bourg and Swaton argue for the view that the conditions for consciousness are embedded in the phenomenal world. Forests, coral reefs, DNA, and the like all "think," they show, in their own way. Human self-awareness is an extension or manifestation of the latent consciousness in all Life. It is an ancient idea that has been resurrected and bolstered with scientific findings by British psychologist Max Velmans as "reflexive monism," a view akin in many ways to the philosophy of "panpsychism." To me those specific formulations are neither here nor there. When, however, Bourg and Swaton urge us to embrace a new paradigmatic relationship to living things, one that reenchants Nature, protects biotic communities as humans are protected with the long arm of the law, yet also affirms the kind of human activity that supports civilized life and leads to more just and stable societies, we are on the same page.

I teach a course called "How to Think about Animals," in which we read T. H. Huxley's classic paper "On the Hypothesis

That Animals Are Automata and Its History," published in the journal *Nature* in 1874. Huxley (1825–1895), nicknamed Darwin's Bulldog for his fierce defense of Natural Selection against the countertide of Victorian sentiment, recounts sympathetically how one of the greatest scientists of the seventeenth century, René Descartes (1596–1650), could have come to the unfortunate conclusion that animals are nothing more than unconscious machines. Against this notion—a logical outcome of an anthropocentric, mechanistic view of Nature—Huxley argues that nonhuman animals are, rather, like us, "conscious automata." While Huxley's conclusions on other matters may fall short of satisfactory, he puts his finger on a button that should signal our attention: consciousness is a real wrench in the works, so to speak. The perhaps irresolvable problem that besets us all, arguably the font and fundament of all our other problems, is that humans are both a part of Nature, yet, with our capacity for recursive thought and symbolic representation, can also stand *apart* from it. We need somehow to reconcile both conditions, what we might call singly the human condition.

Ancient thinkers seem to have understood this dilemma. Their injunction to follow Nature's lead in deciding how to live and what courses of action to pursue is an attempt to resolve it. To the charge that in valorizing this idea from the past I have resorted to cherry picking the evidence I would reply that, well, cherries are delicious. *Of course* we should pick the ripe, low-hanging fruit. And we should preserve it. Some shared, fruitful ideas that I see as worth preserving from the ancient texts discussed in these sermons—works by Lucretius, Plato, Heraclitus, Aristotle, Diogenes, Seneca, and their various epigones like Whitman, Uexküll, Thoreau, Ruskin, and Bataille—are a clarion call to simple, mindful living, a recognition and embracing of natural limits, an affective deference to Nature's organization and natural laws—indeed its awesome beauty—and an underlying nonreductive physicalism, founded on empirical, rational enquiry, that acknowledges unseen realities.

That's a lot of -isms and some sweeping generalizations, I realize. Some may doubt that Plato was a physicalist, or that Diogenes cared a hoot. For my own part I find myself falling back on the worldly wisdom of the human-turned-pig in Plutarch, Gryllus the Oinker, who chastised Odysseus and us all when he declared triumphantly on behalf of his animal brothers and sisters: *"Nature is our whole concern."*

At the end of the monograph in which he presents the *Umwelt* concept to general readers, "A Stroll through the Worlds of Animals and Men" (1934), Uexküll deploys his signature idea to satirize, albeit lightheartedly, his fellow scientists. Each engages with Nature through his or her own limited sensory receptors and morphology—the astronomer explores his universe with the bug eyes of a telescope, the chemist describes hers with an alphabet of elements from the Periodic Table, and so forth. "Soap bubbles" Uexküll calls the various *Umwelten* of this world—ephemeral enclosures with delicate membranes that differentiate one organism from another. The image recalls (unintentionally, it would seem) the Roman agronomist-cum-antiquarian Varro (116–27 BCE), who, in his eighty-fifth year, dedicated a fine guide to agriculture, the *Res Rusticae* ("Country Matters"), to his wife Fundania, who had just purchased a farm of her own: "If humans are bubbles, as the saying goes," Varro apologizes to her in advance of his efforts, "an old man is a bubble all the more."

FIGURE E.1. Jean-Baptiste Chardin (1699–1779), *Soap Bubbles*.

Old or more recent, are the bubbles of our environments impermeable? The very discovery of their existence suggests that they are not. We *can* step outside of our own bubbles to understand other worlds around us. By that same token the capacities that have alienated us from Nature are the very ones that can reinscribe us back into it. Whether we want to live in and with Nature and whether we will ever do so remains to be seen. One thing, however, is certain: bubbles inevitably burst, and when they do, they're gone.

NOTES

Editions of Greek and Latin works are referenced here by volume number in the Loeb Classical Library series (Harvard University Press), abbreviated as LCL.

Preface

Page

xi   The Odgen Nash line, used in the epigraph, from the poem "Come, Come, Kerouac! My Generation Is Beater Than Yours," was published in the *New Yorker* (April 4, 1959). "A Book for All and None" is the subtitle of Nietzsche's volume of parables and sermons *Also Sprach Zarathustra* (1883–1885).

xii   The earlier work of mine to which I refer is *Plato's Pigs and Other Ruminations: Ancient Guides to Living with Nature* (Cambridge University Press, 2020). Parts of this book comprise a fresh development of ideas first entertained in that one and in a few previously published essays, including: "Classics and Complexity in *Walden's* 'Spring'" *Arion: A Journal of Humanities and the Classics* 27, no. 1 (2019), pp. 111–150; "The Environmental Ethics of Delphi: Back-filling Latour's *Facing Gaia*," in *Conversing with Chaos in Greco-Roman Antiquity: Writing and Reading Environmental Disorder in Ancient Texts*, edited by Esther Eidinow and Christopher Schliephake (Bloomsbury, 2025), in press; and "Self-satisfaction," *Aeon*, May 2, 2023. Two books of note that cover related territory differently are Christopher Schliephake, *The Environmental Humanities and the Ancient World: Questions and Perspectives* (Cambridge University Press, 2020), and Graham Parkes, *How to Think about the Climate Crisis: A Philosophical Guide to Saner Ways of Living* (Bloomsbury Academic, 2020).

xiii   In the G. K. Chesterton quotation, from *Orthodoxy* (Dodd, Mead & Company, 1908), p. 85, I have adjusted the word "men" to "people."

xiii   On place-based, relational accountability in Indigenous communities, Shawn Wilson's *Research Is Ceremony: Indigenous Research Methods* (Fernwood Publishing, 2008) is illuminating.

xiv–xv For Longtermism, see William MacAskill, *What We Owe the Future* (Basic Books, 2022) and the profile of the author by Gideon Lewis-Kraus in the *New Yorker* (August 15, 2022). Elon Musk on MacAskill's book: "This is a close match for my philosophy" (twitter.com/elonmusk/status/1554335028313718784?lang=en). For Bankman-Fried, see Craig, Harwell, and Tiku's exposé "FTX's Bahamas Crypto Empire" in the *Washington Post* (November 24, 2022).

xv   "A certain Yogi," of course, is baseball legend and unwitting philosopher Yogi Berra (1925–2015).

xv   The Vauvenargues adage is no. 400 in *Réflexions et maximes* (1746): *Un livre bien neuf et bien original serait celui qui ferait aimer de vieilles vérités.*

xvii   The quotation from Bruno Latour is lifted from *Facing Gaia: Eight Lectures on the New Climatic Regime*, translated by Catherine Porter (Polity Press, 2017), pp. 120–121.

Introduction

Page

1   For Latour's notion of sensitivity see *Facing Gaia*, p. 141.

2   Callicott's thought-experiment is presented in his chapter "Ecological Sustainability" in *The Routledge Handbook of Philosophy of Biodiversity*, edited by Justin Garson, Anya Plutynski, and Sahotra Sarkar (Routledge, 2017), pp. 311–325.

2   The passage of Lucretius that illustrates his point "nothing comes from nothing" is *De Rerum Natura* 1.146–264 (LCL 181). (The Presocratic philosophers Empedocles and Parmenides made a similar argument earlier but did not develop it.)

3   The term "biomimicry" comes by way of Janine Benyus, *Biomimicry: Innovation Inspired by Nature* (Harper Perennial, 2002).

3–4   On the pervasiveness of analogy in ancient thought, see G.E.R. Lloyd's *Polarity and Analogy: Two Types of Argumentation in Early Greek Thought* (Cambridge University Press, 1966), but also, more recently, his *Analogical Inves-*

tigations: Historical and Cross-cultural Perspectives on Human Reasoning (Cambridge University Press, 2015). Douglas Hofstadter and Emmanuel Sander consider analogy the fundament of human cognition in *Surfaces and Essences: Analogy as the Fuel and Fire of Thinking* (Basic Books, 2013). The Oppenheimer quotation is from "Analogy in Science," *American Psychologist* 11, no. 3 (1956), p. 129.

10 The editorial in *Nature* about the need for better climate models by Wei Peng Gokul Iver, Valentina Bosetti, et al., "Climate Policy Models Need to Get Real about People—Here's How" (vol. 594; June 10, 2021, pp. 174–176), inspired just such a model, published in the same journal the following year: Frances C. Moore, Katherine Lacasse, Katharine J. Mach, et al., "Determinants of Emissions Pathways in the Coupled Climate-Social System" (vol. 603, March 3, 2022, pp. 103–124).

12 On the COVID-19 pandemic forcing our hand to rethink our place in the world, see Bruno Latour, *After Lockdown: A Metamorphosis* (Polity Press, 2021), whose title in the original French better suggests the connections to new *oikos*-mentalities: *Où suis-je? Leçons de confinement à l'usage des terrestres* (Éditions la Découverte 2021); the quoted passage comes from pp. 53–54 of the English edition (italics original).

13 "The Great Simplification" refers to a forecast in ecological economics, and the name of a podcast hosted by Nate Hagens (www.thegreatsimplification .com), that, following growth of unprecedented complexity over the past one hundred years, fueled by surplus energy derived from finite resources, human societies will experience an equally momentous contraction over the next hundred as energy becomes scarce and expensive to procure.

Chapter One

Page

14 Descartes's observation (*changer mes désirs plutôt que l'ordre du monde*) comes from *Discourse on the Method*, Third Part.

15 For Epicurean fasting, see the *Epistle to Menoeceus* 131, available in Diogenes Laertius Book 10 (LCL 185) and Seneca Letter 18.9 (quoting from a lost letter of Epicurus to Polyaenus; LCL 75). For Epicurean confession, see W. Schmidt, "Contritio und 'Ultima linea rerum' in neuen epikureischen Texten," *Rheinisches Museum* 100 (1957) pp. 301–327.

16   The *Tetrapharmakos*, from Philodemus = Herculaneum Papyrus 1005, 5.9–14. The Epicurean benediction of Nature = Stobaeus, *Anthology* 17.23 (Frag. 469 in Hermann Usener, *Epicurea* [Teubner, 1887]).

17   Columella on soil depletion = *De Re Rustica*, Preface §1 (LCL 361).

18   The quotation from the Homeric Hymn = no. 30, line 6 (LCL 496); the full text of the Orphic Hymn to Nature, no. 10, is available in *The Orphic Hymns*, edited and translated by Apostolos N. Athanassakis and Benjamin M. Wolkow (Johns Hopkins University Press, 2013).

23   The full title of Liebig's book is *Die organische Chemie in ihrer Anwendung auf Agricultur und Physiologie* (1840), shortened here to *Agricultural Chemistry*. For all matters related to Liebig, see William H. Brock, *Justus von Liebig: The Chemical Gatekeeper* (Cambridge University Press, 1997). The quoted passage is from the 1840 translation of *Agricultural Chemistry* by Liebig's student, Lyon Playfair.

23   On all matters related to plants, see Stephen Blackmore, *How Plants Work* (Princeton University Press, 2018).

25   Liebig's remarks about British bone-gathering appear in *Letters on Modern Agriculture* (1859), no. 11.

26   The first quotation of Marx comes from *Capital*, vol. 1, chapter 10, "The Working Day" (§1); the second = *Capital*, vol. 3, p. 754 (Penguin translation); the third = *Capital*, vol. 3, pp. 949–950.

27   Liebig on *Stoffwechsel* and natural law: *Letters on Modern Agriculture*, pp. 175–177.

27   Lavoisier on the Conservation of Mass: *Rien ne se perd, rien ne se crée, tout se transforme.*

28   The Lucretius passage about properties and accidents = *DRN* 1.450–458.

28   Lucretius's "immortal death has taken away mortal life" = *DRN* 3.869.

28   On Marx's systems ecology, see John Bellamy Foster and Brett Clark, "The Robbery of Nature: Capitalism and the Metabolic Rift," *Monthly Review* 70, no. 3 (2018). In *Marx in the Anthropocene: Towards the Idea of Degrowth Communism* (Cambridge University Press, 2022), Kohei Saito expands on the notion of "metabolic rift" in assessing ecological aspects of Marx's later writings.

29   Aristotle on emergence: *Metaphysics* 8.6 (1045a9–11; LCL 271).

29   The P. W. Anderson essay that articulates the emergence concept without using that word is "More Is Different: Broken Symmetry and the Nature of the Hierarchical Structure of Science," *Science* N.S. 177.4047 (1972), pp. 393–396.

34 The Roman poet Ovid gives the fullest and best-known versions of the stories of Actaeon (*Metamorphoses* 3.138–253) and Erysichthon (8.725–884; LCL 42). See also my discussion of these myths in *Plato's Pigs*, pp. 32–35.

34 Aristotle on the Mean = *Nicomachean Ethics* Book 2, especially 1108b11–13 (LCL 73).

34 The Plotinus passage is *Enneads* 1.6.9 (LCL 440), as translated by Stephen Mackenna (Penguin, 1991).

35 Horace on the Mean = *Sermones* I.1.106–107 (LCL 194).

35 Treaties with Nature: *DRN* 1.584–598. "Divine delight, and a shudder" = *DRN* 3.29ff.

36 The lines from "Song of Myself" come from section 6.

37 Jane Bennett on Lucretius: *Vibrant Matter* (Duke University Press, 2010); on Whitman: *Influx and Efflux: Writing Up with Walt Whitman* (Duke University Press, 2020).

37 The change of tenure at Delphi is recounted in Aeschylus, *Eumenides* 1–8 (LCL 146).

37 The stories from Hesiod come from *Theogony* 126–127, 154–210, and 453–506 (LCL 57).

37 For the navel of the Earth, see Pausanias, *Description of Greece* (LCL 298, plate 76).

38–39 The quotations from *Facing Gaia* are, in order of appearance: pp. 86, 213, 106, 219, and 245 (all italics in the original). For the Gaia hypothesis, see James Lovelock, *Gaia: A New Look at Life on Earth*, 3rd ed. (Oxford University Press 2014; originally published in 1979).

40 Philosophy as a rehearsal for death appears first in Plato's *Phaedo* (63e–65a; LCL 36) and became a philosophical commonplace.

40 For the Mistress of the Animals, see further my *Plato's Pigs*, pp. 18–25.

40 The quotation from Solon is Frag. 36.3–5 (LCL 258).

42 In the quotation from Serres, I have slightly adapted the translation of Elizabeth MacArthur and William Paulson from *The Natural Contract* (University of Michigan Press, 1995; first published in French in 1990), pp. 121–122. Serres's book on Lucretius is *The Birth of Physics*, translated by David Webb and William Ross (Rowman & Littlefield, 2018; first published in French in 1977).

42 Epicurus's will is preserved in Diogenes Laertius, *Life of Epicurus*, 10.17 (LCL 185).

43   Pulitzer Prize for Epicureanism: Stephen Goldblatt, *The Swerve: How the World Became Modern* (W. W. Norton, 2012).

43   On Epicureanism's relevance today, Emily A. Austin's *Living for Pleasure: An Epicurean Guide to Life* (Oxford University Press, 2022) is excellent.

44   The quotations from Roy Scranton are from pp. 115–116 and 109 of his book. Sophocles's so-called Ode to Man, from which I quote = *Antigone* 332–375 (LCL 21).

Chapter Two

Page

45   John Berger's essay, "Why Look at Animals?," originally two separate essays, appears in *About Looking* (Pantheon Books, 1980), pp. 3–28.

46–48   The Aristotle passage is *Parts of Animals* 1.5 (LCL 323), as translated in my book *How to Care about Animals: An Ancient Guide to Creatures Great and Small* (Princeton University Press, 2023).

51   The quotation from William Morris comes from "Hope and Fears for Art" (1882), chapter 3, remarks delivered before the Birmingham Society of Arts and School of Design, February 19, 1880.

51   "Nature does no extra work," or "Nature is not extravagant" = Aristotle, *Generation of Animals* 2.4 739b18 (LCL 366).

52ff.   The passages from Heraclitus (LCL 526) are, in order of appearance: the universe as everlasting fire: D85; fire as exchange: D87; God and incense: D87; wet and dry: D67; empiricism: D31; invisible structure: D50; the sea: D78; the road: D51; beginning shared with end: D54; logos: D46; private understandings: D2; pursue what is shared: R59; the river: A6.

53   Naess articulated the concept of Deep Ecology in "The Shallow and the Deep, Long-range Ecology Movement," *Inquiry* 16 (1973), pp. 95–100.

54   Law of Noncontradiction: Aristotle, *Metaphysics* 1012a24–26 (LCL 271).

56   Uexküll's ideas are summarized in his "A Stroll through the Worlds of Animals and Men: A Picturebook of Invisible Worlds," *Semiotica* 89, no. 4 (1992 [1934]), pp. 319–391; the quotations are from pp. 383 and 326.

62   Nagel: "What's It Like to Be a Bat?" *Philosophical Review* 83, no. 4 (1974), pp. 435–450; quotations from pp. 441 and 448.

63   "Aristotle spurns me" is from Diogenes Laertius, *Lives of Eminent Philosophers* 5.1.2 (LCL 184).

63   The *Cratylus* passage is 439a–440e (LCL 167).

66   Plato's account of *eros*, as related to Socrates by the priestess Diotima, appears at *Symposium* 201d–212c (LCL 166).

67   The systems scientist quoted is physicist Neil Johnson, from his book *Simply Complexity: A Clear Guide to Complexity Theory* (One World, 2009), pp. x–xi.

67   The Sun as an image of the Good = *Republic* 509b1–3; as the offspring of the Good = 506e4; the quotation about the Good = 508e–509a (LCL 276).

68ff. The Participatory Anthropic Principle and U thought experiment are explained by Wheeler in "Law without Law," in John Archibald Wheeler and Wojciech Hubert Zurek, editors, *Quantum Theory and Measurement* (Princeton University Press, 1983). The interview with Wheeler on YouTube can be viewed at www.youtube.com/watch?v=ttestU-obkw. For a favorable estimation of Plato's philosophy for modern physics, see Heinrich Päs, *The One: How an Ancient Idea Holds the Future of Physics* (Basics Books, 2023).

69   Plato's Cave = *Republic* 514a–520a (LCL 276).

72   City for Pigs = *Republic* 369b–376e (LCL 237); the translation of the passage is adapted from the one in my book *How to Be a Farmer: An Ancient Guide to Life on the Land* (Princeton University Press, 2021), pp. 31–53.

73   The quoted passages from the *Statesman* appear at 271c–272d (LCL 164).

74   The quotation of Abram is from p. 138 of his book.

77   For a translation of relevant passages about animal *logos* in Porphyry, see my *How to Care about Animals* (Princeton University Press, 2023).

77   Seneca on following Nature's lead: *De Beneficiis* 4.25.1 (LCL 310).

78   Plato on the dog philosopher: *Republic* 375e–376b (LCL 237).

78   On Stoic *oikeiōsis*, which he translates traditionally as "appropriation," see Christopher Gill, *Learning to Live Naturally: Stoic Ethics and Its Modern Significance* (Oxford University Press, 2022), pp. 151–210, and Jacob Klein, "The Stoic Argument from Oikeiosis," *Oxford Studies in Ancient Philosophy* 50 (2016), pp. 143–200, who speaks of animals' "proprioceptive capacity."

80   Seneca on *oikeiōsis* = Letter 60 (LCL 75).

81   Marcus Aurelius quotations: intercourse: *Meditations* 6.13; *oikeiōsis*: *Meditations* 10.6.2 (LCL 58).

83   Hierocles: The source is Stobaeus 4.84.23; text, translation, and commentary in Ilaria Ramelli and David Konstan, *Hierocles the Stoic: Elements of Ethics, Fragments, and Excerpts* (Society of Biblical Literature, 2009). Circles of Concern graphic and discussion in Kai Whiting, Leonidas Konstantakos, Angeles

Carrasco, and Luis Gabriel Carmona, "Sustainable Development, Wellbeing, and Material Consumption: A Stoic Perspective," *Sustainability* 10.474 (2018).

85 Nietzsche on the Stoics: *Beyond Good and Evil*, trans. R. J. Hollingdale (London, 1973), p. 30.

86 The Henry Beston quotation concludes his reflections in *The Outermost House* (Henry Holt, 2013 [1928]), pp. 217–218.

Chapter Three

Page

88 Camp Fire and Climate Trauma: Gillian K. Grennan, Mathew C. Withers, Dhakshin S. Ramanathan, and Jyoti Mishra, "Differences in Interference Processing and Frontal Brain Function with Climate Trauma from California's Deadliest Wildfire," *PLOS Climate* (January 18, 2023). For the far worse global effects, see Charlie Hertzog Young, "Diagnosing Climate Trauma," *Ecologist* (November 4, 2021).

88 State Farm: Anumita Kaur, "State Farm Won't Insure New California Customers Due to Wildfires, High Costs," *Washington Post* (May 28, 2023).

88 1,000% = Philip B. Duffy, Christopher B. Field, Noah S. Diffenbaugh et al., "Strengthened Scientific Support for the Endangerment Finding for Atmospheric Greenhouse Gases," *Science* (December 13, 2018), vol. 363, issue 6427.

89 For Thoreau the Woods-Burner, see John Pipkin, "Woods Burner: How a Forest Fire May Have Pushed Thoreau to Walden Pond," *Boston Globe* (April 12, 2009), based on his debut novel, *Woods Burner* (Doubleday, 2009), and Robert Sullivan, *The Thoreau You Don't Know: What the Prophet of Environmentalism Really Meant* (HarperCollins, 2009), 212–222.

89ff. All quotations from *Walden* are cited by page number in the edition of Jeffrey S. Cramer, *Walden: A Fully Annotated Edition* (Yale University Press, 2004). "Dull as their readers": Cramer, p. 105; "Deliberately": reading, Cramer, p. 99; living, p. 88. "Delphi and Dodona never gave": Cramer, pp. 98–99.

99 Seneca Effect: Ugo Bardi, *The Seneca Effect: Why Growth Is Slow but Collapse Is Rapid* (Springer, 2017).

101 Leverage Points: Donella H. Meadows, "Leverage Points: Places to Intervene in a System," paper published by the Sustainability Institute (Hartland, Vermont, 1999), pp. 1–19. See, too, Meadows's *Thinking in Systems: A Primer* (Chelsea Green, 2008).

101 For a magisterial overview of systems science, see Fritjof Capra and Pier Luigi Luisi, *The Systems View of Life* (Cambridge University Press, 2014).

102ff. Tom Murphy's "death by hockey sticks" essay appears on his blog Do the Math (www.dothemath.ucsd.edu).

103 For the Planetary Limits article and academic network, see T. W. Murphy Jr., D. J. Murphy, T. F. Love, et al., "Modernity Is Incompatible with Planetary Limits: Developing a PLAN for the Future," *Energy Research and Social Science* 81 (2021), pp. 1–7; for the PLAN network, see planetarylimits.net.

107 Fitchburg Railroad hawk: Cramer, p. 113.

108 "High point of Thoreau's epic": Laurence Buell, *The Environmental Imagination: Thoreau, Nature Writing, and the Formation of American Culture* (Harvard University Press, 1995), p. 170.

108 Cosmos and Chaos: See Ovid, *Metamorphoses* 1.5–7 (LCL 42); cf. Hesiod, *Theogony* 116 (LCL 57).

110 For the contents of Thoreau's personal library, see F. B. Sanborn, *The Life of Henry David Thoreau, Including Many Essays Hitherto Unpublished and Some Account of His Family and Friends* (Houghton Mifflin, 1917), pp. 505–517.

111 Furniture and spring cleaning: Cramer, p. 110.

113 Thoreau's compost: Cramer, p. 3.

114 Thoreau on scale: Cramer, p. 291.

115 The documentary *Manufactured Landscapes* (Zeitgeist Films, 2007), directed by Jennifer Baichwal, is the perfect introduction to the work of Edward Burtynsky.

115 For Krakatoa, see Simon Winchester, *Krakatoa: The Day the World Exploded: August 27, 1883* (HarperPerennial, 2003); the figures cited are from René Dubos, *A God Within* (Charles Scribner's Sons, 1972), p. 163.

116 Nord-Pas de Calais: UNESCO official page: whc.unesco.org/en/list/1360; see also Henri Samuel, "France's Slag Heaps Join Pyramids on List of UNESCO World Treasures," *Telegraph* (July 1, 2012), and Hugh Schofield, "Making a Vineyard Out of Slag-Heap," *BBC News Magazine* (August 4, 2015).

117 For Neri Oxman and the Silk Pavilion projects, see oxman.com. Oxman and her work is profiled in Season 2, Episode 2, of the Netflix series *Abstract: The Art of Design* (2019).

119 Schumacher on appropriate technology: quotation from p. 163 of *Small Is Beautiful: Economics as if People Mattered* (HarperPerennial, 1989 [1973]); larger discussion on pp. 155–201.

119 Kris De Decker and *Low Tech Magazine*: www.krisdedecker.org.

119   The Foxfire books: www.foxfire.org/shop/category/books.

120   Thoreau on clothes: Cramer, p. 23; on shelter and toolbox: Cramer, p. 28.

122   Ancient environmental problems literature began in earnest with J. Donald Hughes's landmark *Environmental Problems of the Greeks and Romans* (2nd edition; Johns Hopkins University Press, 2014), originally published as *Pan's Travail* in 1994.

122   Thoreau on Bias of Priene: Cramer, p. 160; the quotation is from Thoreau's journals, entry dated July 12, 1840.

Chapter Four

Page

125   On Bataille, see Michel Surya, *Georges Bataille: An Intellectual Biography*, translated by Krysztof Fijalkowski and Michael Richardson (Verso, 2010). All quotations come from *The Accursed Share: An Essay on General Economy, Vol. 1: Consumption*, translated by Robert Hurley (Zone Books, 1991).

125   For Ruskin's childhood, education, sexual hang-ups, political views, impact, legacy, and everything in between, *The Cambridge Companion to John Ruskin*, edited by Francis O'Gorman (Cambridge University Press, 2015), is a great place to start, as is UK journalist Andrew Hill's *Ruskinland: How John Ruskin Shapes Our World* (Pallas Athene, 2019).

125   The introductory matter and notes to the thirty-nine volume *Library Edition of the Complete Works of John Ruskin*, edited by E. T. Cook and Alexander Wedderburn (George Allen, 1903–1912), are indispensable.

126   For purposes of tidiness, all quotations of *Unto This Last* are given by essay title and section number, not page number, in Cook and Wedderburn (= volume 17), available online at www.lancaster.ac.uk/the-ruskin/the-complete-works-of-ruskin. However, Clive Wilmer's Penguin edition, *Unto This Last and Other* Writings, might prove more readily accessible to general readers.

126   For a comprehensive introduction to ecological economics, see H. E. Daly and J. Farley, *Ecological Economics. Principles and Applications*, 2nd edition (Island Press, 2011).

127   On the Lindeman publishing snafu: Robert Edward Cook, "Raymond Lindeman and the Trophic-Dynamic Concept in Ecology," *Science*, New Series, vol. 198, no. 4312 (October 7, 1977), pp. 22–26. Lindeman's actual paper is

"The Trophic-Dynamic Aspect of Ecology," *Ecology* 23, no. 4 (1942), pp. 399–417.

128   The Tim Morgan quotations come from p. 11 of *Life after Growth: How the Global Economy Really Works and Why 200 Years of Growth Are Over* (Harriman House, 2013).

131   Aristotle on money: *Politics* 1257a–1259b (LCL 264).

132   "Genital organs of capital": Byung-Chul Han, *Psychopolitics: Neoliberalism and New Technologies of Power*, translated by Eric Butler (Verso, 2017), pp. 3–4.

133   The translation of the Demetrius passage about the phantom economy, from Seneca, *De Beneficiis* 7.1–2, 8–11 (LCL 310), appears in my *How to Say No: An Ancient Guide to the Art of Cynicism* (Princeton University Press, 2022), pp. 37–55.

134   Pound's *usura* poem is Canto XLV.

135   Thomas Piketty's World Inequality Lab and its report: https://wir2022.wid .world; date and time of Piketty's tweet: 3:44 AM, December 7, 2021.

136   Aristotle on *scholē* = *Politics* 1337b27–1338a3 (LCL 264).

136ff.   Quotations from *The Accursed Share*, in order of appearance, "gloriously or catastrophically": p. 21; the calf: pp. 27–28; "our ignorance": p. 23; "greatest orgies of wealth": p. 37; growth limited spatially: p. 29; potlatch: pp. 63–77; "no other diversion" in Tibet: p. 108; solutions to political problems from traditional wisdom: p. 12; relief in festivals: p. 24; the virtues of Tibetan monasticism: p. 109.

142   Seneca on enduring riches: Letter 5.6 (LCL 75).

143   Philo, "every day a festival" = *On the Special Laws* 2.42–48 (LCL 320).

144   Aristotle on the best form of government as most desirable mode of life: *Politics* 1323a-15–17 (LCL 264).

144   Sacrifice as destruction of utility: *Accursed Share*, p. 56; difficulty of implementing *dépense*: p. 40.

144   "At least one degrowth proponent": Onoforio Romano, *Towards a Society of Degrowth* (Routledge, 2020); quotation from p. 71.

144   Julie Livingston's *Self-Devouring Growth: A Planetary Parable as Told from Southern Africa* (Duke University Press, 2019) is a case study of reflections on globalization based on years of fieldwork as a medical sociologist in Botswana.

145   Nuclear weapons cost: Congressional Budget Office on projected nuclear weapons costs: www.cbo.gov/publication/57240.

146   Gandhi on Ruskin: M. K. Gandhi, *An Autobiography, or The Story of My Experiments with Truth: A Critical Edition*, translated by Mahadev Desai (Yale University Press, 2018), pp. 469–471.

148ff.   The foxglove blossom: *Stones of Venice, Volume II*, "The Nature of Gothic" (= Cook and Wedderburn, vol. 10, p. 203); "mathematically not chemically": "The Roots of Honour," §2; the mother and her crust: "The Roots of Honour," §5; balances of justice: "The Roots of Honour," §7; Workers in the Vineyard: Matthew 20:1–16; stealing labour: from "The Work of Iron," published in *The Two Paths* (Cook and Wedderburn, vol. 16, pp. 401–402); Goddess of Getting-on: from "Traffic," published in *The Crown of Wild Olive* (Cook and Wedderburn, vol. 18, pp. 447–448); "the real gist of these papers": "Preface," §2; abstract justice: "The Veins of Wealth," §36; the castaways: "The Veins of Wealth," §§33–35; the middleman: "The Veins of Wealth," §§36–37; "political economists in the true and final sense": "The Veins of Wealth," §28.

156   Hesiod on *kairos*: *Works and Days* 689–694; on its meaning, see R. B. Onians, *The Origins of European Thought: About the Body, the Mind, the Soul, the World, Time and Fate* (Cambridge University Press, 1951), pp. 343–348.

157   Self-sacrifice and voluntary loss: "The Roots of Honour," §§17–25; supply and demand: "Qui Judicatis Terram," §45.

159   Hayek's "The Use of Knowledge in Society," *American Economic Review* 35, no. 4 (1945), pp. 519–530, and "The Theory of Complex Phenomena" (1964), originally published in *The Critical Approach to Science and Philosophy: Essays in Honor of Karl R. Popper* (Free Press of Glencoe, 1964) edited by Mario A. Bunge, are both reprinted in *The Market and Other Orders*, edited by Bruce Caldwell (University of Chicago Press, 2014).

160ff.   "The reddest of the red . . . a Communist of the old school" . . . "violent Tory of the old school": from *Fors Clavigera: Letters to the Workmen and Labourers of Great Britain*, vol. I (Cook and Wedderburn, vol. 27, pp. 122 and 167); needle for a diamond: "Ad Valorem," §67; production as involving "the agency of many lives and hands": "The Roots of Honour," §22; diminishing the power of wealth: "Qui Judicatis Terram," §§51–52. Smart power and the capitalism of the Like button: Byung-Chul Han, *Psychopolitics*, p. 15. Taste as the only morality in "Traffic": Cook and Wedderburn, vol. 18, pp. 434–436; "these are my jewels": "The Veins of Wealth," §41, citing Valerius Maximus, *Memorable Doings and Sayings* 4.4. Preface (LCL 492); "*valor*, from *valēre*": "Ad Valorem," §61; "the manner and issue of consumption": "Ad Valorem," §77; on utopianism: Cook and Wedderburn, vol. 12, p. 56.

Epilogue

171 My account of the word *stock* can be ascertained from the entry in the Oxford English Dictionary.

171 Pliny the Elder's comment about *pecunia* appears at *Natural History* 18.3.11 (LCL 371).

172 Aristotle on natural slavery: *Politics* 1254b16–21 (LCL 264); Aristotle on women: *Generation of Animals* 737a25 (LCL 366).

173 On Herbert Butterfield and Whig history, see Ernst Mayr, "When Is Historiography Whiggish?" *Journal of the History of Ideas* 51, no. 2 (1990), pp. 301–309.

173 For Protagoras's dictum, see Plato, *Theaetetus* 152a (LCL 123). The whole of it, purportedly the first sentence in his lost book titled *The Truth*, reads: "Of all things the measure is the human being: of those things that are, that they are; and of those that are not, that they are not."

174 Bourg and Swaton's book has not yet been translated into English. Here is the French of the passage I summarize as concordant with my own thinking, from *Primauté du vivant: Essai sur le pensable* (Presses universitaires de France, 2021), p. 230: "Nous avons ainsi cherché à réenchanter, à réanimer le monde, et pourtant nous ne sommes en quête d'aucune restauration, d'aucune volonté de retour au passé. D'un côté, la pensée mechanist a donné des fruits inestimables, et au premier chef les droits humains, même s'il convient désormais de les completer par les droits de l'humanité et de les insérer au sein de l'ensemble plus large des droits de la nature; elle a également provoqué un arrachement historique de sociétés entières à l'extrême pauvreté, vis-à-vis de quoi il va falloir redéfinir un standard matériel et de confort compatible avec le maintien de la vie sur Terre. De l'autre côté, c'est l'élan même de connaissances impulse par le mécanicisme qui a conduit à son propre dépassement. En outre, ce réenchantement intervient au seuil d'une dynamique de degradation accélérée de conditions climatiques de l'épanouissement de la vie sur Terre, et en plein effrondrement de cette même vie."

174 For reflexive monism, see Max Velmans, *Understanding Consciousness* (Routledge, 2000). Bourg edits an online magazine *La pensée écologique* (lapenseeecologique.com) and Swaton runs Fondation Zoein (zoein.org), both outreach ventures that promote ecological lifestyles and policies in Europe.

174   On panpsychism, the seminal paper is Thomas Nagel, "Panpsychism," in his book *Mortal Questions* (Cambridge University Press, 1979), pp. 181–195. A more recent formulation of the same idea by Philip Goff, which he calls "cosmopsychism" is developed in *Why? The Purpose of the Universe* (Oxford University Press, 2023).

175   Huxley's essay from *Nature* (September 3, 1874, pp. 362–366), expanded and revised, appeared also in the *Fortnightly Review* of the same year (vol. 22, pp. 555–580), where is added, famously, the author's own tentative view of human consciousness: "The soul stands related to the body as the bell of a clock to the works, and consciousness answers to the sound which the bell gives out when it is struck."

176   The references to Uexküll are from the beginning and end of his monograph.

176   For bubbles in Varro, see *Res Rusticae* 1.1 (LCL 283).

INDEX

Note: Page numbers in italic type indicate illustrations.

Abram, David, 73, 74
Adams, Ansel, 115
Aesop, 45
agriculture. *See* farming
Ainsworth, Robert, *Latin Dictionary*, 110
Alcott, Bronson, 122
alienation, 14, 45, 130–31, 177
All-India Spinners Association, 118–20
ammonia, 33
analogical thinking, 3–5, 181
the ancients. *See* Greco-Roman cultures
Anderson, P. W., 29, 114
animals: behavioral stimuli for, 57–60; consciousness/rationality of, 77, 174–75; expenditure of energy by, 136–37; as guide to human values and behavior, 46, 77–82; humans in relation to, 45–50, 62; proprioceptive capacity of, 79–82; scientific study of, 46–50; *Umwelt* of, 56–60
animism, 74–76
Anthropocene, 9, 38, 43, 98, 174
anthropocentrism, 173–74

Apollo (mythological figure), 34, 37–38
Aristotle, 11, 29, 34, 46–51, 54, 59, 63, 77, 85, 131–32, 136, 143–44, 148, 153, 162, 172, 175
Arts and Crafts movement, 146
asceticism, 15, 93
Atlee, Clement, 146
atoms/atomism, 2, 11, 14–16, 18, 27–28, 43
Attenborough, David, 61
Aztecs, 140

Bankman-Fried, Sam, xv
Bardi, Ugo, 99, 101
Bataille, Georges, 125–26, 136–42, 144, 167, 175
Baths of Diocletian, Rome, 39–40, *39*
beauty, 34–35, 48, 51, 65, 66, 148, 176
Bennett, Jane, 36–37, 42
Berger, John, 45–46
Berra, Yogi, xv
Beston, Henry, 86
Bias of Priene, 122–23
biomimicry, 3

biopolitics, 163

biosphere, xiv, xvii, 5, 9, 38, 53, 84, 98, 139

Blake, William, 33

Bohr, Niels, 55

Book of Numbers, 142, 144

books, 89–90, 146. *See also* ideas

Botticelli, Sandro, *Venus and Mars*, 18

Bourg, Dominique, 174, 191

Britain, 24–27

Buddhism, 45, 77, 140–42

Burns, Robert, 37; *To a Mouse, on Turning Her Up in Her Nest with the Plough*, 26–27

Burtynsky, Edward, 115

Butterfield, Herbert, 173

Caesar, Julius, 17

Callicott, J. Baird, 2–3, 11

Camp Fire (2018), 87–88

capitalism, 26, 28, 45, 132, 161, 163–64, 166–67. *See also* money; wealth

catallactics, 160–61

Cedar Bog Lake, East Bethel, Minnesota, 127

chance, 14–15

Chancel, Lucas, 135

change: Heraclitus and, 52–53, 63; in human affairs, 100, 104–5; in Nature, 13, 63–64, 100, 104–5; Plato on the concept of, 63–66

chaos, 108–9, 121

Chardin, Jean-Baptiste, *Soap Bubbles*, 177

ChatGPT, 29

Chaucer, Geoffrey, 97

chemistry, 23–27

Chesterton, G. K., xii–xiii

Chicago, motto of, xvi

Chicago School of economics, 159

chickens, 59–60

Cicero, 153

Citizens United v. FEC (2010), 160

classics. *See* Greco-Roman cultures

climate emergency, 6, 8–11, 13, 137

climate trauma, 87–88, 115

closed-loop systems, 2–3

Club of Rome, 32, 101, 130

coal, 33

colonialism, 161

Columella, 17

community: Plato's conception of the ideal, 71–73; Ruskin's conception of, 150; Stoic conception of, 82

complexity science, 50, 52, 67, 109, 114

compost, 3, 12, 17, 19–21, 23–24, 113, 138. *See also* fertilizers; manure

consciousness, 174–75

conservation of energy, 3

conspicuous consumption, 140

Corn Laws (Britain, 1846), 25

cosmopolitanism, 95, 143

cosmos, as order, 108–9, 121. *See also* universe

cosmovision, 74–76

COVID-19 pandemic, 12

Cronon, William, xvi

Cynics, 92–98, 121, 132–33

Dalai Lama, 142

Daly, Herman, 130

Darwin, Charles, 175

death: certainty of, 15, 39–40, 40, 43, 104–5, 113; life in cycle with, 19–24,

27–28, 36, 112–13; as nothing to fear, 15; as part of Nature, xii, 12–13, 28, 40, 43–44, 112

De Decker, Kris, 119

Deep Cut, 117

Deep Cut (Fitchburg Railroad line), 108–9, 114–15

deep ecology, 53–54

deepfakes, 29

degrowth, 144

Delphic Oracle, 34, 37–39

Demetrius, 95–96, 132–33

Democritus, 27

denuclearization, 145

Descartes, René, 14, 175

desire, acquisitiveness, and consumption: adverse effects of, 9–10, 80–81, 95–96, 143; ancient injunctions against, 121–22; Bataille on, 136; moderation of, 14, 93–94; philanthropy and, xiv–xv; psychopolitical uses of, 163–64; Ruskin on, 167–68. *See also* wealth

Diogenes of Oenoanda, 15–16

Diogenes the Cynic, 92–93, 97–98, 121, 123, 175–76

DNA, 50, 174

Domus Aurea, Rome, 110–11

Dyce, William, *King Lear and the Fool in the Storm*, 9

ēthos (habitat, disposition), 79

Earth: agricultural practices harmful to, 25–26; Delphic Oracle and, 37–38; energy expenditures on, 137–38; Epicurean concern for, 16–18; future of, 12, 103–4; humans'

impact on, 16–17, 95–96, 103–4, 124, 129, 174; life-death cycle on, 19–24, 27–28, 36; limits of, 103–4, 139. *See also* biosphere; climate emergency; Great Mother; Nature

ecological economics, 125–26, 128, 162–63

ecology: beauty and, 51; coining of the term, 56; deep vs. shallow, 53–55; etymology of, 11, 50, 78; Heraclitus's thought and, 53–55; and Nature as home, 11; of systems, 28, 50, 53; trophic levels in, 126–28, *128*, 136; *Umwelt* concept in, 56–62, 82. *See also* Traditional Ecological Knowledge

Ecology (journal), 127

economy: adverse impacts of, 124; Bataille's theory of, 136–44; as energy circulation mechanism, 2, 126, 128–30; etymology of, 11, 153; exalted by modern societies, 124–25, 151–52, 158–60, 168; inequalities in, 134–35; misconceptions of, 124–25, 130; money's role in, 128–31; Nature as guide for, 125; purpose of, 124, 155, 158; Ruskin's critique of, 148–58, 160–63, 166–68; self-organization imputed to, 158–61; sociopolitical expenditures of surplus from, 144–45. *See also* capitalism; ecological economics; wealth

Effective Altruism, xiv–xv

Effie Gray (film), 145

Einstein, Albert, 55

electromagnetic spectrum, 60–61, *61*

Elton, Charles, 126

emergence, 29

Emerson, Ralph Waldo, 89

Empedocles, 180

empiricism, 3, 16, 50, 53. *See also* sense experience

Enclosure Movement, 25

energy: animals' expenditure of, 136–37; Bataille on expenditure of, 136–42, 144; economy as circulation of, 2, 126, 128–30; as limited resource, 103; Nature's expenditure of, 127–28, 128, 136–45; premodern adumbrations of the concept of, 3, 52; Sun as source of, 2, 12, 66, 127, 129

Energy Research and Social Science (journal), 103

Engels, Friedrich, 26, 28–29, 114

entropy, 12

environment. *See* ecology; Nature; *Umwelt*

Epicureanism, 2, 12, 14–16, 28–29, 35, 36, 42–44, 114

Epicurus, 4, 15, 27, 40, 42–43

ethics and morality: absent from Nature, 85–86, 113–14; animal behavior and, 79–80; Delphic sayings as guides to, 34; Epicureanism and, 2, 43; etymology of, 79; of human-Nature relationship, 43; Ruskin and, 164; Stoicism and, 79–85. *See also* human values and behavior; justice

eudaimonia (happiness, flourishing), 83–85, 84

Euripides, *Bacchae*, 34

evolution: human's place in, 90; Nature's plan and, 59; proprioception and, 79–81; sensitivity to environ-

ment as necessity for, 1; timeline of Earth's, 91

excess. *See* desire, acquisitiveness, and consumption; energy: Nature's expenditure of; "nothing in excess"

excrement, 110

extraction industry, 96

Facebook, 49

farming, 20–27, 30–33

Fénelon, François, 122

fertilizers, 23–26, 30–33, 138. *See also* compost; manure

Fitchburg Railroad, 105–8, 106. *See also* Deep Cut

food chains, 127–28

Forcellini, Egidio, *Lexicon*, 110

Forster, E. M., *A Room with a View*, 146

Foucault, Michel, 163

Fourteenth Amendment, 160

Foxfire (anthologies), 119

freedom, 159–60, 163

Gaia, 37–39

Gaius Gracchus, 165–66

Gandhi, Mohandas, xv, 118–20, 146–47

Gleason, Herbert Wendell: *The Fitchburg Railroad and Walden Pond in Winter, Concord, Mass.*, 106; *Sand Foliage from Deep Cut on R.R. (Railroad), Concord, Mass.*, 107

Goldilocks Principle, 30

Gracchi, 165–66

Gray, Euphemia, 145

Great Mother, 40

Great Simplification, 13, 181

Greco-Roman cultures: and economics, 131–33; environmental impact of, 121–23; and living with Nature, xiii; Ruskin and, 153, 166–67; Thoreau and, 90–92, 121; value of studying, xi–xii, 172–73, 175–76

Greece (ancient), 34, 37, 40

greenhouse gas emissions, 33

The Green Planet (documentary), 61–62

grotesques, 110–11

Haeckel, Ernst, 56

Hagens, Nate, 181

Haida, 140

Han, Byung-Chul, 132, 163–64

happiness. See *eudaimonia*

Hardin, Garrett, 10

Haudenosaunee, 75

Hayek, F. A., 158–63

Heisenberg, Werner, 55

Heraclitus, 47–48, 51–56, 59, 63–66, 77, 109, 113–14, 175

Herodotus, 79

Hesiod, 37–38, 79, 108, 155–57

Hierocles, 83–84

High Farming, 25–26

hockey-stick curves, 102–3, *103*, 134–35

Hofstadter, Douglas, 181

holism. See whole systems

Homer, 45, 79, 90–91, 107

Homeric hymns, 18, 36

Horace, 35, 153

Hubble Telescope, 61

humanism, 173

humanities, 10, 44

humans: achievements of, 44; alienation of, from Nature/animals, 14, 45, 130–31, 177; death as certain end of, 15, 39–40, *40*, 43, 104–5, 113; DNA shared with other living things, 50; limitations of, 61–66, 69–71; Nature in relation to, xvi–xvii, 1, 9, 14, 45–46, 75, 90–91, 124, 175; and the nonhuman world, 45–50, 62, 74; technology in relation to, 119; universe in relation to, 5, 62, 64. *See also* human values and behavior; knowledge

human values and behavior: animals as guide to, 46, 77–82; as cause of climate emergency, 9–11, 13; the Cynics and, 93–98; deep ecology and, 55; ecological, 11, 46; Epicureanism and, 14–16, 42–43; ideas as supreme among, 71; Indigenous values and behavior and, 76; irrational character of, 10–11; the mean as a standard for, 15, 34–35; Nature as guide to, 2–6, 11–13, 16, 28, 35, 42, 73, 77–82, 93–94, 142–44, 175–76; peace of mind as goal of, 3, 14–15; preparation for disasters, 100–101, 104–5; proprioceptive, 79–82; Ruskin and, 166–67; science in relation to, 43; the Stoics and, 77–85, 104–5; tradition as guide to, 11. *See also* ethics and morality; humans

humility, 39

humus, 23–24, 39

Huxley, T. H., 174–75, 192

Ideas (Platonic Forms), 64–67, 71

ideas, supreme value of, 71. *See also* books

Illich, Ivan, 119

India, 118–19, 146–47
Indigenous peoples: and animals, 45; expenditure of surplus energy by, 140–42; harms suffered by, 75; and living with Nature, xiii–xiv, 73–76
Industrial Revolution, 33
instinct, 59
Islam, 140

Jataka Tales, 45
Jevons, William Stanley, 33
Jevons Paradox, 33
justice, 78, 150, 152–55, 162. *See also* ethics and morality

Kimmerer, Robin Wall, 73
knowledge: limitations of, 61–66, 69–71; Plato's conception of, 64–73; quantum mechanics and, 67–69; sense experience's role in, 64–71; *Umwelt* concept and, 56–62. *See also* science
"know thyself," 34, 39–40, 39
Krakatoa, 115–16
Kropotkin, Peter, xiii
Kwakiutl, 140

language, 64–65
Latour, Bruno, xvii, 1, 3, 12, 38–39
Lavoisier, Antoine, 27
Law of Noncontradiction, 54
Law of the Conservation of Energy, 3, 37
Law of the Minimum, 30–32
Leigh, Mike, 145
leisure, 136, 145
leverage points, 101–2

Liebig, Justus von, 23–27, 29–33, 44
Liebig's Law/Barrel, 30–34, *31*
life, as source of value, 166–68
Like button, 164
The Limits to Growth (report), 32, 101, 130
Lindeman, Raymond, 126–27
Linnaeus, Carl, 11
literacy. *See* writing
Livingstone, Julie, 139
logos (reason, measure, account), 55–56, 64, 77, 79, 98. *See also* reason
Longtermism, xiv
Lovelock, James, 38
low-tech, 118–20
Low-Tech Magazine, 119
Lucretius, 2–4, 6–7, 9–11, 13–18, 21–22, 27–29, 36–37, 40, 42–43, 175
Lyon, Rome, 99–100, 104

Machado de Oliveira, Vanessa, 76
manure, 17, 24, 137–38. *See also* compost; fertilizers
Marcus Aurelius, 81–82
Margulis, Lynn, 38
markets. *See* economy
Marmite, 24
Marshall Plan, 140
Marx, Karl, 26–29, 44
Material Ecology (exhibition), 117
Mauss, Marcel, 140
Meadows, Donella, 32, 101–2, 104
mean (middle point), 15, 34–35, 156. *See also* "nothing in excess"
Merleau-Ponty, Maurice, 74
Meta, 49–50
metabolism, 27–28

metaphysics, 49, 55, 63

methane, 136–38

Metroön (shrine), 40

Michelangelo, 110

Mill, John Stuart, 126, 148, 166

Millais, John Everett, 145

Mistress of the Animals, 40, 41

moderation. See "nothing in excess"

modernity: adverse impacts of, 9–10,
    56; alienation characteristic of, 14,
    45; conundrums of, 75; writing as
    catalyst of, 76. See also mean

monasticism, 142

money: abstract thought linked to,
    130–31; critiques of, 131–34; eco-
    nomic role of, 128–31; etymology
    of Latin term for, 171; as means of
    exchange, 131–32, 136. See also capi-
    talism; desire, acquisitiveness, and
    consumption; wealth

morality. See ethics and morality

Morgan, Tim, 128–29

Morris, William, 50–51

Mount St. Helens, Washington, 116

Mr. Turner (film), 145

Murphy, Tom, 102–3

Museum of Modern Art, New York, 117

Musk, Elon, xv

Naess, Arne, 53–55

Nagel, Thomas, 61–62, 66

Nash, Ogden, v

National Parks (United Kingdom),
    146

National Trust (United Kingdom),
    146

Natural Selection, 175

Nature: agency in, 59; alienation of
    humans from, 14, 45, 130–31, 177;
    amorality of, 85–86, 113–14; ancient
    peoples' lives in relation to, 1–2;
    change in, 13, 63–64, 100; concept
    and terminology, xv–xvii, 38, 173–74;
    consciousness in, 174–75; consola-
    tion provided by living in accordance
    with, 3, 15; Cynics' conception of,
    93–94; as guide for the economy,
    125; as guide to human values and
    behavior, 2–6, 11–13, 16, 28, 35, 42,
    73, 77–82, 93–94, 142–44, 175–76;
    humans in relation to, xvi–xvii, 1, 9,
    14, 45–46, 75, 90–91, 124, 175; inter-
    relationship of all things in, 3, 26–27,
    38–39, 50, 52–55, 66–67; Law of the
    Minimum in, 30; life and growth in,
    20–27, 30–35, 36, 49, 112; limits in,
    30–35, 176; Lucretius on, 2–4, 6–7,
    9–11, 13–18, 21–22, 27–29, 36, 42;
    Marx and Engels on, 26–29; mecha-
    nistic conception of, 173–75; pur-
    pose in, 48, 51, 59; resilience of, 13,
    21, 108, 115–17, 123; Ruskin and, 148,
    158; sensitivity to, 1, 3; Stoic concep-
    tion of, 77–86, 98; Thoreau and, 105,
    108–15; unity of, 6, 53–56, 113. See also
    climate emergency; Earth; reality;
    universe

Nature (journal), xv–xvi, 10, 175

neoliberalism, 164

Nero, 110–11

nettles, 32

New Materialism, 37

Newtonian physics, 77

Nietzsche, Friedrich, 85–86, 98, 114

Nord-Pas de Calais, France, 116

"nothing comes from nothing," 2–3, 6–9, 12–14, 21–22, 27–29, 36

"nothing in excess," 34, 80. *See also* mean

nutrient cycling, 127

oikeiōsis (making familiar or akin to oneself), 78–84, *83*

oikonomia (house-management), 131, 153

oikos (household), 11, 78

Oppenheimer, J. Robert, 4–5

Orphic hymns, 18, 42

Ovid, 108–9

Oxman, Neri, 117–18, 120; Silk Pavilion II, 117–18

Oxo, 24

panpsychism, 174

Parable of the Cave (Plato), 69–71

Parable of the Workers in the Vineyard (Gospel of Matthew), 150

Parmenides, 180

participation, 64–67, 76–77

Participatory Anthropic Principle, 68, 69

Pausanius, 37

Phidias, 40

Philodemus, 42–43

Philo of Alexandria, 142–43

Piketty, Thomas, 134–35

PLAN (Planetary Limits Academic Network), 103–4

plant growth, 20–27, 30–33, 36

Plato, 63–73, 76, 78, 153, 155, 175–76; *Cratylus*, 63, 65–66; *Republic*, 66, 71–73, 78, 153; *Statesman*, 73; *Symposium*, 66

Platonism, 43

pleasure, 15, 92–93

Pliny the Elder, 171

Plotinus, 34–35

Plutarch, 94, 176

Poggio Bracciolini, 43

Porphyry of Tyre, 77

potlatch, 140, *141*

Pound, Ezra, 133–34

Pre-Raphaelite movement, 146

presentism, 4, 90

Prigogine, Ilya, 29

Propp, Vladimir, 19

proprioception, 79–82

Protagoras of Abdera, 173, 191

Proudhon, Pierre-Joseph, 28

psychopolitics, 163–64

public wealth, 135

quantum mechanics, 67–69, 71, 77

Raphael, 110–11

rationality. See *logos*; reason

reading. *See* books

reality, sense experience in relation to, 64–71, 77, 176. *See also* Nature; universe

reason: animals' use of, 77; the Cynics and, 98; role of, in living with Nature, 56; Stoic conception of, 81–82. *See also* ideas; *logos*

recycling, 2

reductionism, 62, 104, 173

reflexive monism, 174

relativism, 54–55

relativity, 54–55
Reynard the Fox (medieval tale), 97
Ricardo, David, 126, 148
Rome (ancient), 17–18
Ruskin, John, 125–26, 145–69, 174, 175; "Lectures on Painting and Architecture," 168; personal seal and motto "To-day," 169; *Self-portrait in Blue Neckcloth*, 147; *The Stones of Venice*, 148; "Traffic," 151; *Unto This Last*, 146, 148–50, 153, 156, 158, 161, 164–65; "The Work of Iron, in Nature, Art, Policy," 151

Sandburg, Carl, "Grass," 21
Sander, Emman, 181
sand foliage, *107*, 108–10, 114
scholē (leisure), 136, 145
Schumacher, E. F., 118–19
science: and contemporary animism, 76; environmental footprint of, 118; human values and behavior in relation to, 43; individual fields' perspectives and practices in, 176; limitations of, 62–63; Lucretius/Epicureanism and, 3, 16; as means of understanding Nature, xvi, 3, 5; reductionism in, 62, 104, 173; and study of animals, 46–50. *See also* knowledge; technology
Scranton, Roy, 43–44
Seaford, Richard, 130–31
Second Law of Thermodynamics, 128
self-preservation, 75, 80–81
self-sufficiency, 93–94
Semper, Karl Gottfried, 126

Seneca, 77, 80, 82, 95, 99, 104–5, 123, 142, 175
Seneca Curve, *102*
Seneca Effect, 99–102
sense experience, reality in relation to, 64–71, 77, 176. *See also* empiricism
sensitivity, 1, 3
Serres, Michel, *The Natural Contract*, 42
Seven Sages of ancient Greece, 122
Shakespeare, William, *King Lear*, 6–11, 13
sheep, 60
silkworms, 117–18
simplicity, 43, 72–73, 92, 121. *See also* Great Simplification
slavery, 160
smart power, 163–64
Smil, Vaclav, 35
Smith, Adam, 126
socialism, 163
Socrates, 40
solar energy, 2
Solon of Athens, 40, 122
Solow, Robert, 130
Sophocles, 44; *Oedipus Rex*, 34
Soviet industrialization, 140
Spall, Timothy, 145
Sprengel, Karl, 24
State Farm Insurance, 88
stock, meanings of, 171–72
Stoics, 77–86, 98, 142
Stoppard, Tom, *The Invention of Love*, 145
subtraction, growth by, 34–35
Sun, 2, 12, 66–67, 127, 129
sustainability, 2–3, 84, 101, 134, 138, 145
Sustainability (journal), 84

Swaton, Sophie, 174, 191
systems science, 50. *See also* whole
systems

technology: appropriate/low-tech,
118–20; disconnectedness from
Nature due to, 1; ecological costs of,
5, 33; environmental footprint of,
118; extraction industry needed to
supply materials for, 96; humans in
relation to, 119; limitations of, 10,
32–33; surplus energy produced by,
139; world as created by, 75; writing
as, 74. *See also* science
TEK. *See* Traditional Ecological
Knowledge
terrils, 116
Thales of Miletus, 122
Thomas, Elizabeth Marshall, 73–74
Thompson, Emma, 145
Thoreau, Henry, 89–92, 97–98, 105–15,
117, 120–23, 168, 175; "Economy," 113,
120, 168; "Sounds," 107, 111; "Spring,"
108–9; *Walden*, 89–91, 97, 105, 108,
122, 168; "Walking," 112
thought. *See* consciousness; ideas;
reason
Tiberius Gracchus, 165–66
Tibet, 140–42
ticks, 57–58, *58*, 60
Tlingit, 140, *141*
totemism, 45
tradition, xii–xiv. *See also* Greco-
Roman cultures; Indigenous peoples
Traditional Ecological Knowledge
(TEK), 73–75
tragedy of the commons, 10

Trajan, 111
Trophic Pyramid, 126–28, *128*, 136
Turner, J.M.W., 145
2001: A Space Odyssey, 29

Uexküll, Jakob von, 56–59, 62, 71, 85,
175–76,
Umwelt (environment), 56–62, 71, 79,
82–83, 176
UNESCO World Heritage sites, 116
United Nations, 6
universals, 64
universe: change in, 13; human knowledge of, 44, 61, 68; humans in
relation to, 5, 62, 64; materialist
conceptions of, 14–15, 37, 43.
See also cosmos; Nature; reality
US Department of Defense, 145
US Department of Energy, 145
US Supreme Court, 159–60
usury, 133–34
utopianism, 168–69

Valerius Maximus, 165
values. *See* human values and behavior;
life, as source of value
Varro, 176
Vauvenargues, Marquis de, xv
Veblen, Thorstein, 140
Velmans, Max, 174
Venus (mythological figure), 18, 42
Voltaire, xv

Walden Pond, 89–90, 105–8, *106*,
114–15
wants. *See* desire, acquisitiveness, and
consumption

war, as expenditure of socioeconomic and political excess, 139

Watt, James, 33

wealth: accumulation of, xv, 131–32, 149; critique of pursuit of, 142–43; inequalities in, 134–35; life as, 166–68; as power, 164–65; public, 135; Ruskin on, 153–57, 162, 164–68. *See also* desire, acquisitiveness, and consumption; economy; money

Webb Telescope, 60–61, *61*

Wheeler, John, 68, 71

whiggery, 172–74

Whiting, Kai, 84

Whitman, Walt, 113, 175; "This Compost!," 19–23, 36–38, 43

whole systems: and emergence, 29; life-death cycles in, 13; relationship of parts in, 5, 48, 51–54, 82; study of, 48, 50. *See also* participation

Wilde, Oscar, 146

wilderness, xvi

wildfires, 87–89

Wittgenstein, Ludwig, 64

World Inequality Lab, 134–35

writing, 65, 74, 76

Xenophon, 153

Yong, Ed, 56–57

zoos, 45–46